SMALL TALK

Poems New & Selected

OTHER BOOKS BY PETER SEARS

Green Diver (CW Books)

The Brink (Gibbs-Smith Publisher)

Tour (Breitenbush Books)

I Want to be a Crowd (Breitenbush Books)

CHAPBOOKS

Luge (Cloudbank Books)

Icehouse Beach (Chowder Chapbooks)

The Lady Who Got Me to Say Solong Mom (Trask House Books)

Bike Run (Raindust Press)

SUPPLEMENTARY TEACHING TEXTS

Gonna Make Me a Rainbow Poem (Scholastic, Inc.)

Secret Writing (Teachers and Writers Collective)

SMALL TALK
Poems New & Selected

PETER SEARS

A Northwest Masters Series Book from

LYNX HOUSE PRESS
Spokane, Washington

The *Northwest Masters Series* is comprised of *New and Selected* volumes by distinguished poets living in, or principally associated with, the Pacific Northwest, including British Columbia. Responsibility for publication of titles in the series is shared between Lynx House Press, of Spokane, Washington, and Lost Horse Press, based in Sandpoint, Idaho. Titles in the series, to date, include:

The Book of Shadows Carlos Reyes (Lost Horse Press, 2011)
Built to Take It Tom Wayman (Lynx House Press, 2014)
Small Talk Peter Sears (Lynx House Press, 2014)
To Love That Well Robert Pack (Lost Horse Press, 2014)
Habitation Sam Hamill (Lost Horse Press, 2014)

Northwest Masters Series | Christopher Howell: Editor

FIRST EDITION

Cover art: Chit Chat by Simon Bull. Other fine paintings by Simon Bull may be viewed online at www.bullart.com.
Author Photo: Angela Schwindt.
Book & Cover Design by Christine Holbert.

LYNX HOUSE PRESS books are distributed by the University of Washington Press, 4333 Brooklyn Avenue NE, Seattle, WA 98195-9570.

ISBN 978-0-89924-136-4

Library of Congress Cataloging-in-Publication Data is available from the Library of Congress.

to Anita

TABLE OF CONTENTS

Small Talk: New Poems

from *Green Diver* (2009)

from *The Brink* (2000)

from *Tour* (1987) & *I Want to be a Crowd* (1979)

Small Talk: New Poems

LATE NAP

I take a long hot tub so that I can feel like a melon.
I dry myself off and tingle like a coral reef.
The lower sheet I pull tight. I puff the pillows,

lie on my back, stretch out my arms and legs.
If I'm lucky, a breeze sweeps in sweet as silk.

The sleep is calm, like a coin at the bottom
of an old fortress wall that protrudes into the sea,
and the coin is almost green from the slow sloshing.

In the sleep, nobody comes after me, I don't
have to go anywhere, and I am immortal.

THE PROBLEM WITH BEING A PALLBEARER IN THIS CITY UNDER SIEGE

The problem with being a pallbearer here
is that you get shot at.
The same guys who sit in peace negotiations
sit in the towers
and shoot at our funeral processions.
We hear them laughing.
We hold the casket to shield us
and shoot back.
Down from the towers they come for a lunch break.
When they drive through the neighborhood,
they drive fast, trying to hit people.
When we catch one of them,
we tell him that not long ago
we put a buddy of his in a casket
and carried him through the streets, by all the towers.
Maybe you shot him, we say.
Maybe you hit him.
Now we are going to put you in a casket
and carry you through town.
You've got breathing holes in the bottom of the casket.
That's where the blood runs out.
When you guys see blood running out,
maybe you think you shot a crate of tomatoes.
When was the last time we saw tomatoes?

AT THE OLD CEMETERY OUTSIDE OF FOSSIL

The wind in the trees on the other side of the field
slides across into the poplars on my side
and drives the cold deeper into me.
I huddle and try again
to read the name on the cemetery stone.
Someone used the stone for target practice.
It's about all that is left of the cemetery,
and the cemetery is about all that's left of town.
The place feels a little snakey,
as if I'm trespassing.
A whirl of wind stands up in the field, about my size,
and whirls my way. It leans to the left
and then to the right. I get the feeling
it wants to dance with me.

OCEANS OF KANSAS

Daughter, remember how you love Kansas, because of Dorothy,
and I told you that millions of years ago
Kansas was underwater—
the whole state an ocean full of fish and seaweed,
and you cried crazy? I said, I'm sorry, Kansas is fine now.

Days later you were still drawing pictures of houses underwater
and long hoses down to the houses
and machines on the sides of the houses to pump the air in
and people with helmets on with little hoses
and fish swimming into the refrigerator and out
before you could shut the big white refrigerator door.

I show you how to draw a refrigerator with the door open
and fish swimming in and out at funny angles.
You keep crying a little as if you have forgotten why,
and turn your head away
and draw and draw.
You say we have to keep drawing
if we are going to stay alive underwater in Kansas.

PETALS

There you were in the first X-Ray slapped up on the office wall.
"See," the doctor said, pointing at you with his cue,
gingerly, as if not to arouse you.
Cancer tumor, you looked like a doughnut
—no, more like an igloo—
but you had not begun to spread. "So we'll get right in there,"
the doctor said, "and operate on that tumor"

—as if I was going in with them, in with the doctor and nurse,
to see you up close,
touch you, watch you be sliced out of my lung,
then dropped in a dish. Then what? Tossed in the garbage?
Put in an urn?
I look up again at the X-Ray slide; I could swear
your clean borders have shifted,
have begun to leak.
"We'll try to get you into surgery within the week," the doctor said.

This morning, on my way to the hospital, April petals
float at the traffic light while I wait
for the red to turn to green,
petals so light they glance off the traffic light,
back into their slow flowing.

I ask you, cancer cells, did you come to me
like these morning petals
and fall and drift on to other cells?
Tell me, did you pile willy-nilly like snow, or did you float and fall
and grow into obedient rows,
building, building, row house after row house?

THE OLD WOODS

As a kid I learn the woods are spooked, so when I go in,
I make piles of pinecones, cake them with mud,
and place them through the woods.
I'm small. Small is good for hiding. I walk
in the woods, too—I wait to feel something watching me,
maybe even following me,
to scare me, to see if I spook and run.
What I like to do is step off the trail into the underbrush, wait,
covered up like a bush ball, and see what comes by
and where I might be
if I was still walking. I might catch sight of the dead
and spook around them,
slip up behind one of them, and make him flutter
and get caught in the branches and tear himself.

I dream of being in the woods again with the dead and the owls
and my pinecones. Then I lose the dream.
I wait for it to come back to me as if I have gone ahead
and have to wait for myself to catch up.
Days later, I wake early. Light is coming up,
I watch it rise behind the trees.
This is before dogs and cats and kids,
before anything looks like anything I can trust. It's so early
turkeys are floating down in the dark
from the tall trees where they sleep.
They don't fly down, they drop,
slowly, like tents swaying, a half dozen of them
pecking the ground and another half dozen
standing in the middle of the street, twitching their heads.

MORNING LIGHT

I'm here on the deck, blowing on my coffee,
watching poppies open slowly in the morning light,
one orange cup after another. They help me forget
that my stomach floats in my throat, here in week three,
round two, of my chemo. I have to remember to eat
and that, in my mind, I am not always all here. I stand
—I've learned about the dizzies—and imagine myself
strolling down a flagstone path which I'll build next spring
after the rains. I look forward to the quick spring light
glinting off the flagstone that I will lay one stone at a time,
on my knees, on an old cushion, with a deep stack
of stones to choose from. This stack I will call
my little ziggurat. I sip my coffee. The morning light
is still too heavy to lift over the hills into our back yard.
Yet the poppies continue to open their orange cups,
one after another, around their black stamens.
My coffee, I'll sip it, then take a full, luscious swallow.

HI MOM, PLEASE PICK UP

Hi Mom, please pick up, I'm coming home tonight late,
so please turn off the alarm. I don't want to wake you. Remember
the time I got there late and had to ring you up and you didn't pick up
and I slept on the lawn and those people came by tipsy and sang out?
    Look at creepie on the lawn. He's not dead.
    He's just got rattles in his head.
I hate being called creepie.
So I really hope you get this. Frankie says you're not there any more.
Janie says maybe you're dead. That's not nice.
I know you like to keep the lights off to keep folks from prying.
Do you remember my setting you up with a dead bolt?
That wasn't so long ago. If you have some chores for me,
just leave a note. I'll sleep downstairs and not bother you.
In the morning, I may be gone before you awake,
so let me thank you now.

I HUM TO MY SHIVERING

I am walking along the road at night,
shivering, humming to my shivering.
I walk into a spider web in a doorway

—that's what it feels like. I wave
my hand across my face. Snow!
I've caught it just as it starts.

It smells good. Maybe things will
be okay. I worried all day. I couldn't
keep anything down. Look,

the snow seems to part as if
opening up a passageway.
Is that how it feels going over

to the other side? When I go,
maybe I'll dissolve like one of
these snow flakes. I look up into

so many against the night. Flakes
land in my palm one at a time.
I feel like a happy old god.

DAD, TELL ME

Dad, tell me that you bent down and picked me up,
held me high and kissed me on the cheek,
nuzzled your bristly cheek into my little cheek
and turned me slowly so that I could see the world.

Tell me that you sat down across from me
at my level and talked to me and asked me
what I had done that day and what I thought
and felt and what I might like to do.

Years ago the doctor said, "Stop drinking
and smoking." You sat in your chair, watching TV,
drinking and smoking, and when the programs
ended late at night, the screen went to static

and fizzed, I was in the doorway behind you
the night you got up and went over to the TV,
stuck your finger on the screen, tapped
and said, "Fuzz, fuzz, I'm ready to go."

Trying to remember if you were ever there for me
is like walking up to a room, feeling along the wall,
in the dark, for a light switch, and starting to step in
before I'm sure there is a switch, a room.

PLEASE EMPTY YOUR POCKETS

Is that everything?
We don't want anyone to think you may not be entirely forthcoming.
This coin of yours is very old.
Perhaps it will bring you good luck. We like to say that we get you in
and get you out, but the truth is reviewing takes time
and there can be snags,
sometimes for no apparent reason.
You needn't be afraid, yours is a routine check.
We can't be too careful,
the citizens have been hurt too many times for us not to be
extremely careful. To tell you the truth, we are a little afraid of the citizens.
We came in the back door just now.
One time one of the janitors took this table. That chair you are sitting in,
someone took that too, another time,
and brought it back, scorched. It stank until we painted it black.
It's hard to feel secure.
Relax, we'd be suspicious if you didn't have things in your pocket,
like this jackknife and rabbit's foot,
and if you weren't a little nervous, as you seem to be now.
Please turn your pockets inside out
and put your hands on the table.

HEY CHUCK

These guys keep saying, Hey Chuck this and Hey Chuck that.
My name's not Chuck. They are family, too. Come on, they could
get their jollies somewhere else. They take me fishing
because I'm so bad they can blame me for the fish not biting

—or just to fun me. Maybe I try too hard, like the time I flipped
my line to make a big cast, caught it in a tree, pulled,
slipped on the bank, and fell in. Then once we waded out
in big boots, my boots filled up. They laughed, I almost drowned.

I have a cousin, though, who's nice. She invited me
for a sweet at the art museum coffee shop. I walked around
the rooms with her. Those German expressionists, that's
what she called them, they were wild, like a brand new animal.

I couldn't help but stop by this one painting of a cockeyed,
rake-thin, orange lady with a blazing head of big red hair.
Reminded me, I said, of when I was lighting my Zippo lighter
near a lady with shiny hair spray and her hair caught fire.

So what do you think of the painting? My cousin asked.
. . . I like it, the painter must have had a special feeling
for her and painted her. I get those feelings sometimes.
. . . Would you like to paint me? My cousin asked.

. . . Why would I want to do that? . . . You could paint me any way
you wanted, my cousin said, however you felt about me.

THE NEWT

The nurses roll us out here behind the clinic
for the afternoon sun, you like a mummy on a flatbed,
me like a car salesman in a lounge chair,
but I don't mind because the newt may come out to warm himself
here on the porch steps,
which is chancy, what with the birds.
I shoo them away, the cats too.
I like the little guy.
He can appear and disappear, he's that fast.
Hey friend, under all that wrapping, you haven't seen the newt yet,
have you? Maybe you'll see him today,
but you have to try,
you have to open your eyes.
I bet he's got one of those lickety-split tongues.
I'd like to see him in action, you know, take a bug out of the air.
We could have a contest: you, me, and the newt.
The newt would win.
The nurses have been nice to me lately.
That's not a good sign.
Maybe I don't have much longer.
Then there's the newt. What's going to happen to him?
You look like you're wrapped for shipment,
and I'm not too sharp either.
I'm about as much fun as an old magazine.
Maybe he won't come out until everyone has left.
That's what I would do.
But we're here for a while,
he likes these porch steps, and it's warm.

BACK FROM WAR

It's nice to have our son home again.
We worried every day, especially when he didn't call.
He's back now from Afghanistan

with a pretty bad concussion,
but he has his music, games, and computer upstairs.
It's nice to have our son home again.

You may have seen him in his fatigues downtown.
He was good about looking for work
when he first came back from Afghanistan,

but his concussions were too bad. He was begging
the other day—said he was just going out to get some air.
Still, it's nice to have our son home again,

even if he's on lots of medications
while we wait for the VA to say he's getting better.
At least our son is back from Afghanistan.

Please, if you see him downtown begging,
point out the bus stop and write down the right number,
and tell him it's nice to have him home again,
that you're glad he's back from Afghanistan.

PLANE DOWN IN MORICHES BAY

I didn't know what my brother meant
when he said the sound of the explosion
reached our town, and he still didn't know
what had exploded when he and the other volunteers
gathered uptown, before dawn, and drove west,
to Center Moriches, to the bay,
where wreckage of a huge plane
sprawled across the night gray waters.
Volunteers waded into the shallow bay,
my brother said, formed lines,
held both hands out to the man in front of them,
bending over at the waist, their elbows dipping
into the water. What was passed to each man
each man passed on: a piece of fuselage,
a piece of corpse, a broken lobster pot
long on the bottom. They stepped gently,
all the volunteers said so. Some said
there was too much debris in the water
for the souls to rise off the bay.
You do not look at the man in front of you,
it was hard enough to keep your face quiet.
What helped, the volunteers said,
was to take deep breaths and let them out slowly
across the water. A couple young guys
said they felt souls in the water.
They were led back to shore.
Now and then, the volunteers in the lines
looked out across the bay to the inlet

and out to the ocean where the sun
was coming up—but not for long
for fear of not being ready
when the man in front turned to them
with something in his arms.

LONG AFTER I AM GONE

Some day my daughter will make a left turn,
long after I am gone, and think of me,
not because she sees something in particular;

no, and not because of an odd overlap like
a rowboat crossing the path of lake moonlight,
but because I just rise in her memory like toast;

yes, she and I in a Laundromat, feeding tumbles
of quarters into the dryers' silver mouths
to make all five dryers spin long enough

to get ornery blue jeans dry as crackers.
"Do you see yourself there in the Laundromat?"
"Yes, Dad, I'm running from dryer to dryer,

sticking in quarters *kerplunk kerplunk,*
but I guess I'll go back to putting stickers
on my school notebook because this is taking

a lot longer, Dad, than you said it would."
This recalling what you said helps me now
against each day falling faster and faster away.

EVEN IN HADES THEY TALK TURKEY

I

Odysseus resents retirement. He storms around the house,
throwing brochures of Mediterranean cruises
and declaring, "If you are not on deck but, instead,
down in those decadent glitz rooms, how can you smell
the shifts of wind?" Penelope, doing yoga exercises
on the living room floor and having recently
talked Odysseus out of signing up for a special forces reserve unit,
sends him to a writing conference with three rules:
he may not go around bare-chested
or slaughter local livestock, and he must call home each evening.

At registration, he admits he has no writing.
"Still I insist on being in the memoir workshop. This time
I'll tell my own story." When advised that workshop placement
is determined by staff, Odysseus says that he is having
Athena T-shirts flown in for everyone.
"Athena who?" asks a staffer. Odysseus sighs.

He brings no writing to class, but is enthusiastic.
"I love everybody's writing, even the ghoulish tale
of the two young girls who set out in a rowboat without oars
and, in a fit of self-pity, throw themselves overboard."
When asked why, he quotes from the piece, "The way the waves
break on the shore like whispers."
The screenwriting teacher, overhearing him, exalts,
"With a voice like that you could hail the gods."

Odysseus adds, "I do, but do they listen?"
and wanders off to what he calls "the trees and wine
where as long as there is wind, there is someone to talk with."
Staff and conference attendees stare at one another, agog.

II

The person Odysseus hangs out with calls herself Electrique.
From her headstand on the main building porch,
Electrique says to Odysseus, "Don't think about what you write,
just pour it over your head."
Odysseus replies, "You make me want to practice knife throwing."
Electrique comes to the evening reading dressed,
as she says, "in the spirit of the panther," followed by Odysseus.

After the reading, everyone gathers at the bar.
Odysseus says, "The main reader reads as if he was the official
palace scribe." Electrique adds, "More like a would-be king."
"He did mention phantom pain," says Odysseus,
"which I took to mean the pain of phantoms, and it's true
that when wraiths appear, they always seem to be in pain."

The bartender shouts, "Mr. O, they are trying to close up the bar."
The conference people listening and scribbling furiously,
but pretending not to, get up to leave.
Odysseus stands and says, "You know, phantom pain

may be pain we can't identify
because it's from a life before.
So it's not available to us, unless we visit Hades."

"Hurry up please, it's time," says the bartender,
and everyone shuffles about, except Odysseus,
who says to the abandoned space, "I tell you, there is a time
before dawn when it is still dark;
I wake up, I can't sleep, and walk around, excited,
as if there is a scrambling before the light.
When I talk like this, Penelope tells me
to double-check my meds and not eat before I go to bed."

III

Odysseus never does write anything for the workshop,
so no one expects him to take part in the student reading.
He gets a hold of the sign-up sheet
and places himself last, and Electrique in the middle.
He doesn't want to follow Electrique,
she reads too well. He places next-to-last
a tone deaf young man who shuns complete sentences,
is into theory, will read too long and, if gonged,
will become hostile, sweat profusely, and read much longer.

By the time Odysseus steps up to the podium,
the crowd is crazy happy. Odysseus says,
"I am trying to mix language, space, and water,
and make sentences light enough to float across water.
They will float if they come from song."
Even the post-modernists love this.

Odysseus pours water over his head and sings.
Electrique crouches in the main aisle. The crowd leaps up
and much damage ensues.
Odysseus continues to sing.
The next morning he apologizes as he writes a check
and explains to the staff that he has been a bit unruly
because "I have long been into doing, not writing."
"Writing is doing," says Electrique.

"Tell me then," he asks, "Do you think I have to understand
what I am going to write before I write it?"
"Not at all," she replies.
"Put that on your evaluation," suggests a staffer.
Odysseus sighs and looks out to the parking lot
where people are hugging and loading up their cars.

Turning to Electrique, Odysseus says, "You know,
it drives me a little nuts, this always yearning a little,
not about anything in particular. Just that nudge.
So I spend much of my time
looking around, picking up things and putting them back down.
I love it, I'd have it no other way."

HARD

I hang at the high school bike stands and lock my bike and then, pretending not to like my spot, unlock my bike and move it to another spot and lock it up again. I do this a couple of more times to come to homeroom with her already in her seat up front so that I can pretty much stare at her the whole homeroom period without anyone noticing. My friends, if they find out, will razz me. So I am careful sneaking good looks at her, like I'm putting a cape over her and drawing her to me saying things to her that I can't even hear.

After homeroom, I probably won't see her again until after lunch. That's O.K. Lunch is dicey, sitting with my friends, who gawk around, crack dirty jokes, and guffaw. So that means I don't see her until Latin, sixth period. She's terrible at Latin. When she is asked to translate, I just die. She doesn't know anything. I doubt she cracks a book. I love Latin. I love her. If only I could save her, swoop her up in my arms and carry down the hall to, like, shop or study hall, or maybe right out to the ball fields, murmuring Latin love words. That way she wouldn't understand a word and would have to ask me what I'm saying. I'd just smile. But maybe I can't carry her that far, she is bigger than I am.

In Latin, when I am called on, I try not to speak too enthusiastically. I don't want everyone thinking I am doing it for her. I am doing it for her. I do everything for her. Have you heard of the ablative absolute? Well, that's what the Latin teacher asked her about. She sat there. I wanted to stand up and shout, Ask somebody who knows! Like me! Ask me! But I cowered there, for her, for me, for everyone crushed by an ablative absolute. We don't even have the ablative case in English. The teacher is just mean.

I should be grateful, I guess, I am not in any of her other classes. English class could be worse because when they didn't have enough copies of *The Merchant of Venice*, they switched to *Romeo and Juliet*. What if I had to read Romeo when she read Juliet? I'd commit suicide. Well, pretty close. What if someone else got to read Romeo when she read Juliet? I'd hate him, I'd challenge him to a duel and he would probably say, "You're crazy," and my friends would laugh their asses off. I'd like to ask Romeo about his baggy pants and what about dancing with Juliet, pressing her to him?

What I'd really like is to get taller. Coach asks me about it. We have this play where I set a screen for the other guard, but I'm so short the guy guarding me can just reach over me and block the guy's shot. So I don't get to go in for that screen play anymore. I'm sent in now only to foul guys, to keep our starting players from fouling out. The ref likes to yank my jersey up to see my number and holler it out. He says he'll call a technical foul on our team if I can't keep it tucked in. I don't believe him, he can't be that mean, but coach believes him. Coach likes to say, "I ask you to take one foul, not two," and look around as if he just made up the dumb joke.

I would much rather keep my jersey tucked in anyway because, when it hangs down over my shorts, it looks like I only have a shirt on. That's what my friends say, laughing their asses off as usual. The cheerleaders look away, embarrassed for me. I could die. But I can get up and down the court faster than anyone. They call me Butterfly. They call me Speeding Bullet. They call me Winger. I dribble too hard, the ball comes up too high. I outrun the ball, but one thing about playing: I don't worry about what my crazy body is doing.

The problem is I don't get into the game very often—maybe every third game—and just long enough to foul some guy, who looks at me as if I'm a jerk. So most of the time I am sitting on the bench. When coach calls your name to go in the game, he leans over and shouts it down the bench to paralyze you. It paralyzes me. I have to stand up. What if I have been thinking of her and getting a little crazy if you know what I mean? I have to lean over and rush up along the bench to the coach. I lean down on one knee to get instructions—you know, like which guy to foul—and then I slide over to the scoring table, check in, lean down on one knee and pray. I don't look down.

If she were at the game, I wouldn't care if I didn't play a second. There are always the warm-up drills, she'd see me. I could wave. I wouldn't do that, though. And if I did get to play, I'd play much better with her cheering. I could whisper to her later that she had inspired me. She probably wouldn't believe me, but I could smell her breath and her hair and try to store it in my memory.

Cheerleading tryouts are coming up. I hope she tries out. I know she would make it, she's so pretty. But maybe not. A friend of hers told me that she is not trying out because she thinks cheerleading is dumb—where is her school spirit?—and she doesn't want to go to all those away games, and she can't jump, and she doesn't want to learn the dumb cheers. Heck, you learn them by hearing them all the time. She'd be a gorgeous cheerleader. I can see her on their bench, that skirt, that sweater, those little white sneakers. Makes me dizzy.

I dream of her waiting for me after practice and, sure, walking home together. I would probably be aching big time pretty much the whole way and trying not to show it, you know, just talking and walking slowly carrying her books and not looking down.

Once I speak to her, that's it. She will know I like her and tell her friends, and then everyone will know. I might as well carry a sign around, but I sure would be proud to be her boyfriend. I would hate people asking me questions about us, though. I want to say that before I respond, I'd like to talk with her about it first. Then they might think I wasn't much of a guy.

What I'd really like is to hang around and talk with her as if we were just hanging around, but I don't know how to do that. I mean, what do you say when you don't have anything to say? Some guys are good at that. They talk to girls a lot, the popular guys. They just go around being popular. My life isn't like that. I go to class, I have my friends, I go to practice, I do my homework, and I take care of my bike. Sometimes, I'm called to the principal's office to help with some sorting. The secretaries are nice to me. I don't know much of anything else. I know what happens, though, when I think of her. It hurts.

DEAR GIANT SQUID

This is a fan letter. I don't care what the scientists say,
I saw them on TV getting all excited about how they have photos
of you and almost caught you by dropping juicy bait down to
the creepy depths where you live, along with a fancy camera.
Next time, eat the camera. Their footage shows you approaching
the bait and taking it and getting caught, then dragging the line
up and down, around and around. When you finally ripped yourself
free, you lost a tentacle, which they dangled on a post as if
they had been down there fighting you with their bare hands.
What a joke! You would have wrapped them—right?—and popped
their eyeballs out. So now you know they won't quit until they
get you. They will scrounge more money and more cameras
and more bait and more boats because that is the way
humans are, most all of them some of the time and some of
them all of the time. So you had better head down, way down,
and don't wise off and try to take on some whale. A drawing
in a book when I was a kid showed a whale as black as the black
sea it dove down through, with its jaws open over most
of the tentacles of a giant squid, just like you, and the whale's
eye right up next to the giant squid's eye. Made me sick.
I turned the page, then turned back, I couldn't help it,
those jaws closing on so many tentacles, about to chop them
like so much spaghetti. That's how we humans are, bloodthirsty,
even when we are young and small and not so mean yet.
There is a lot about us not to like. The scientists won't rest
until they lift you breathless out of the water and lower you
into a cage, take lots of measurements, speak in low, earnest
voices to the eager public, and shake hands all around.

BORNEO

Boycott my funeral and tell everyone not to come.
Tell them the funeral is a sham, that just a week ago
you saw me in Borneo in the jungle. I didn't look great,
maybe, but who looks great in the jungle? I was in a hurry
and said I would meet you at the hotel, in the lobby,
in those big hard-cushion chairs. I know they don't call it
Borneo any more. Those folks arranging my funeral,
ask them what's in my coffin? Rocks? Rocks and worms?
Remind them you just saw me in Borneo, and I looked
healthy enough. You've got to be in good shape to be
in the jungle. You and I, we paused outside the hotel
and watched the light come down through the branches
on to the ferns. You recall that I suggested we stroll out
on to the veranda for a round of those spiked iced teas
to toast the moon dripping up over the tall bamboo
and wonder if the world really is still at war.

HIS FRIEND THE BEAST

The man likes being friends with his beast,
his only companion. His family complains
about the beast. That gives the man headaches.
He wants to scream, but good men don't scream
at their families. Sure, the beast stinks. Sure,
he shouldn't let the beast come inside and sleep
in the hallway, but he doesn't have the heart
to drag him out. His family wants to cut the beast's
liver out, have friends over for dinner. He doesn't
want to think about that. He wants to think big,

think up ideas that will help everybody, like
planting many crops instead of few. His family
whines; they won't guard many crops against
the animals. Too dangerous, they insist. Why don't
you make the beast do it? And how can you put
your family in harm's way? For the work they
contribute, he thinks, they might as well be
puddles. All they talk about is the great old days
in the caves that talked back to us. He curses them
with nightmare and falling out of trees. All day
he works hard and falls asleep on top of his wife.

She cries, says he's heartless as a crow.
Does he even remember his children's names?
He can't think when she yells at him. He looks
across the field where crows complain all day
and still seem to enjoy themselves. The wind

sweeps the grass. He inhales the scent of
the grass. I'll do anything, he says to himself,
not to slaughter my beast. I love my beast
more than my family. If I could only find
some happy seeds to suck on
to help me forget for a while. He belches.

The beast says, Why don't we walk around
and smell things, then lick the ones we like
or lie down in them? You are not a crow,
you are a burdened man. If you listen to your
family, they will have you slaughter me.
I'll know and I'm much quicker than you.
I'll kick you in the groin and tromp you until
your teeth crack. Your mouth, that belch hole,
will become deep red as a plum. I'll tell
my fellow beasts. They'll take turns leaving
their gaze on you like a shadow. You'll be
alone. You've never really been alone.

DEAR GIANT SQUID, #2

I am trying to decide if it's worth signing up for the Mars colonization trip. Probably not—too old, too shot. Anyway, I'd miss my wife, my daughter, my cat. Oh dear, here's another show on TV about Giant Squids. Can't we just leave them well enough alone? This time it's in the Sea of Cortez.

You squids, listen up, they will attach a camera and a long, long line to a small squid and drop it into the water. Down, down, it drops to where you live. Now they have photos of one of you big guys chomping on a little squid. They couldn't see all of you. But they could see your eyes,

so they measured the distance between your eyes—and that way measured your size. Over 60 feet. A record. That's not good. It's got these humans really excited. The next time you see a camera, eat it. The photos on the tape they'll show over and over and get more excited.

That's the way we humans are. Get an idea and we gnash on it until we go nuts, like dogs gnashing on a stick. You don't have dogs, sorry, but maybe you've got fish that chase seaweed or something until they go nuts. Or you go nuts watching them. Or you don't go nuts at all

because only we humans go nuts. That might explain a whole lot of things. As for being there in the Sea of Cortez, where you've been gliding around for millions of years, you've got to leave. Hey, do you think we like the idea of colonizing Mars? Well, maybe some

humans do, but they are not well adjusted and suffer probably from massive illusions of grandeur no matter how well they score on the tests. We are colonizing because we are frying this planet and sooner or later we have to vamoose. Here's the thing though, you can't go outside on Mars. If you do, you fry, and if you stay inside too long without gravitational pull, your bones go. You don't know about bones because you don't have them. With us gone, though, you would have the oceans all to yourself if there are any oceans left.

THE RAIN SOUNDS LIKE A DELICATE EATING

You wake to rain, roll over, and let the softness fall
out of the bottom of your brain.
You wake again, later, to rain, and slog into the day,
out the front door, down on to
the flagstone path by the ivy and the Doug firs dripping.
Can you hear a drop strike a leaf of the ivy?
Yes, you think you can.
You see a leaf flutter.
You look from one struck leaf to another, and another.
The moments between drops
are like lighter leaves under darker leaves.
You listen to what you call "front rain" and "back rain."
Front rain is what you hear,
back rain is what you think you hear, what you want to hear.
The rain on the ivy, you say to yourself, is like a clicking,
like a delicate eating.

Standing water you like too,
and hearing rain strike standing water.
Rain may carry back to you something you had forgotten
or hadn't thought of in a while,
particularly soft rain.
What of rain that blows out of trees,
down the back of your neck,
making you laugh and wrinkle your neck?
And yet you say you don't really like rain. It's too beguiling,
you don't believe it. What do you mean
you don't believe it?

I believe that when I hear a poem,
I hear the silences between the words.
Like rain. I hear the intervals
between rain striking leaves or standing water.

THINKING OF CALLING MY DAUGHTER

Sometimes I think there is not enough time to tell my daughter
everything I want to tell her so that I can live through her memory.
She will re-create me as she chooses. When she recalls something
I don't remember and joyously reminds me, I'm speechless.

I pull in for gas. The teenage girl with acute acne and scrizzly hair
is being teased by her mother, who is smoking and waiting
for her car, up on the lift. The girl pleads with her mother to stop
teasing her. Which seems to please her mother,
who teases her more and worse and laughs and smokes.
The girl screams louder, beats her hands on the sides of her head.
Her face tears apart into laughter and tears.

I work on my breathing. Sunlight bakes the field where the hay
has just been cut. I could drive back by at dusk and maybe see a fox,
maybe a family of foxes, the father and mother pouncing,
trying to teach the two little kits how to pounce. The kits try,
they just roll over. The parents look away. The kits try again.

I doubt there will be foxes here at dusk and if there are,
probably I won't be able to see them.
Here in my car, I'm trying not to think how bad the war is.
Even when it's over, it won't be over.
There'll always be a "protective force"—that's the invasion idea—

and the American compound may outlast the pyramids.
I'm not getting any nicer either. When the little foxes fail to pounce,
because they are still too young,
the parents don't punish or nag them. They sit there, alert.

DREAM OF FOLLOWING

with a nod to David Romtvedt

I am following my father and mother,
following them although I don't much like
the idea, and I don't much like

that the distance to them grows smaller,
so small I'm catching up to them. You'd think
we'd have much to say to one another.

We don't. My father motions me
to look back over my shoulder.
There's my daughter following me.

That's mean of him. I want to hail her,
tell her to slow down.
But I don't. I turn back, they're gone.

LIKE A SPOT IN THE WOODS WHERE DEER SLEPT

The mermaids ease into the pool
without getting their hair wet.
They stretch and soften in their syncopations.
See the happy bubbles from their kicks.
The cameras roll and because their scaly mermaid costumes
have not been tested for their weight the mermaids sink.

My mother was one of the mermaids.
My father shot down a fast stream,
bobbing up from time to time between the rapids,
with his golf club aloft whirling.
At the end, when he popped up, he was waist high
out of the water, gasping, his ruddy face spread out like a shovel.

Daughter, I tell you these dreams of my mother and father
because one day soon
I may seem to you like dreaming.
Let me brush your hair in back where you can't see
and it gets spun funny and flattened
like a spot in the woods where deer slept.

I TURN MY EMAIL OFF

for Anita

I turn my email off to get away from thinking away, away.
I turn my computer off to leave the braining of screens and files.
I remove my hearing aids
so that I won't hear the phone.
I take my glasses off
so that I can read no print.
I take my teeth out so that I cannot talk.
I take my feet off and put them carefully in the sock drawer
so that I won't go for a walk.
I take my fingers off
and lay them on the side table
so that I cannot take up a pen and set the brain a-buzzing.
I put my stumpy hands on either side of my head,
squeeze and release,
squeeze and release,
to turn my pulsing head into something like a pumpkin.
I drop my breathing down to a pond with no wind on it.
Then, when I close my eyes,
I can hold still
my thought of you.

THE OLD DEMON DROPS BY TO COOL OFF

I think because we were the last spread
heading out of town toward the mountains,
the old demon would stop by and cool off

in our pool. He could lie on the bottom
for minutes at a time, curled, like a sack
of meal. In the evenings, when things cooled

under a hundred, he'd lie on his back on
the surface, the hairless pinhead of his,
and his wings spread out—he looked like

a manta ray. I don't know what that stuff
was around his mouth. Drool maybe.
Anyway, splat, he lands in the pool

and not all that gracefully. The old demon
starts in about the obnoxious young
demons chasing him out of downtown.

He says I'm afraid
        I'm a little frayed
         around the edges.

Later, lonely at the kitchen sink,
washing yesterday's dishes,
waiting for my kids, I find myself

saying I'm afraid
        I'm a little frayed
        around the edges.

I tell my kids not to turn their backs
on him and not to pull the metal chairs
across the stone terrace by the pool.

That could send anyone around the bend.
They've been playing out there, I'm sure,
when he was spread out in the pool.

But what can a mom do? My crazy kids,
they like to run into the house
and dance around the kitchen table

singing I must confess
        I'd like to mess
        with you.

He never has. He might favor us
because the only time we saw him out
of the pool was when Big Mike was over,

doing his house fix-ups just fine until,
into his second six-pack, he hollered hard
at the kids for calling him "Big Bad Mike—

they were actually saying "Big Mac Mike"
—and splat, the old demon is across
the window, his back to us, and slowly turns

around, to face Mike, his wings out,
the tips twitching. You couldn't look
at him for long. Mike didn't and was gone

in a clatter. When we sold the place
and moved up here into the hills, we didn't
see the old demons again. The kids still

like to say I must confess
                I'd like to mess
                with you.
You can't blame them.

YOU WEREN'T THERE

You weren't there when dad came home that night
and stood in the middle of the living room
like he was the rocket at Cape Canaveral
going into the final countdown.
If smoke had seeped out
from under his pants, over his shoes,
along the floor of the living room,
curling around the banister where I stood,
I would have believed it.
If I had taken one step into the room,
I probably would have stepped on
an invisible downed power line
and electrocuted both of us.
You're lucky you weren't there.
I'm lucky you weren't there
because when you get afraid,
you say crazy things
like the time you asked him, "Do you want to kill us?"
Remember how we could hear his breathing
through his teeth? Remember
how his eyes got thin?
This time he just stood there.
Hours later, when he came back,
he said nothing, as if it hadn't happened.
That made me crazy,
I wanted to hit him.
Maybe that's what he wanted all along.
It might have been all he needed.

MY FOUR PITCHES

My first pitch is a fastball which I grip with two fingers
on the laces and release in a flat, downward motion
so that the ball, spinning more, may dance a little.
I like calling it my split-finger fastball or splitter.

My second pitch is a curveball for which I grip
half the ball and break off the motion at the release
so that I am staring at my palm with my two little
fingers turned in. The ball breaks to the left,
away from the righthanded hitters.

My third pitch is a screwball which I grip with
the fullness of my hand and I bring my arm down
in the release, turning my hand under to the left.
The ball bends to the right, in on righthanded hitters.

My fourth pitch, a knuckleball, I grip with my knuckles
and release with almost a push so that the lack of spin
allows the ball, at the whim of the air, to wobble.

My knuckleball doesn't wobble, doesn't do anything.
My screwball I can't throw because it hurts my arm.
My curveball breaks more than my screwball,
and if I throw it from about three quarters it bends
to the left and down, but often starts bending
well before the plate, what they call a roundhouse,
and batters sit on it, smash it into next Tuesday.

I have no sinker, no slider. My fastball doesn't dance, doesn't do anything, and it isn't fast. That's why I play in the infield. When no one else is free, I get to throw batting practice. The guys say my speed is just right.

LUGE

I love snow, long gone now from the valley,
but still patching and striping the Cascade
Mountains and beyond the front ridge, the
white triangle of Three-Fingered Jack shining.
Makes me want to try out for luge. They hold
tryouts around the country—who knows,
there might be a senior circuit. I love the high
 banking in the turns as if the luge is going to
shoot off the track. Perfect for me: push off
and pray. The motion at the start when you grip
the handles and sway back and forth in place,
that I already do. I do that on the floor with
my cat, watching a ball game. I'm not sure
whether you steer with your hands or with
your feet. How do you hold on, though, through
the tunnel racket and see where you are going?
If you look up, you lose speed. If you don't
look up, you may go over the bank into a tree,
and bye bye bye swaying snowbird spirit.
As you soar over the tops of pines, your life
may flash before you—or maybe nothing,
nothing but pines coming up at you. Yet
if you keep the luge right side up, you might
drop into dry snow, burrow a bit, and emerge
to slide down a long ravine where a team of folks
making a movie about—well now maybe they
have a real story—swirl around you like moons,
shove a mug of coffee into your blue hands,
and badger you about your deft touch.

from *Green Diver* (2009)

MY EMPTINESS RIDES IN THE BACK SEAT, PROPPED UP

Don't look now but that's my emptiness smiling at us
from the back seat of the car with the hat on that's too small.
I give him hats that fit and he chucks them out the window.
Then flops over, face down,
probably laughing his eyeballs out. I prop him up.
Maybe I should get him like a baby chair.
Or tape him to the back seat.
Yesterday he caught me looking at him
in the rearview mirror.
That smile, I can't take it.
I threw fresh mints back over my shoulder at him
as hard as I could.
I threw the towel at him that I use to wipe the windshield
and almost piled into a Dodge 4x4.
That's it. I stop the car, take him out, sit him
on a wooden bench in the park, and walk back to the car.
Yeah, just leave him there.
He's my emptiness, I can do what I want with him.
He's such a baby. Maybe he should have to do it on his own.

Well, I barely get around the block
when I whip the car around and head back for the little whuss.
I mean, how long can he last on his own?
So I am getting out of my car
when I happen to glance at the back seat.
There he is, my emptiness, with one of those dumb hats on,
waving my car keys.

CHEMO SILVER

Think of silver, liquid silver dripping into your veins
from sacks dangling above your chair,
like lungs breathing in, breathing out,
while goldfish here in the chemo clinic aquarium
pucker on the glass
and scented candles nauseate the room,
the room of tiny killings,
benign cell, cancer cell,
leaving your kidneys the chewed socks of God.
O sperm of death, O sweet sweat of aluminum,
you take my body from my being
and make me a dirigible of fizz.
Liquid silver, moon juice, I suck you in.
Chemo limo, I ride you through the bends.

WE CAN HELP EACH OTHER

See, I remember you said your darkness
was waking you up at night and not letting you

go back to sleep. And I want to hear
more about your darkness, really.

I can help you. We can help each other.
Why don't you ask me about my darkness?

You know I want you to. Se let me
tell you again: I'm driving along

when darkness shoots up in front
of me as if the hood of my car

flew up in front of the windshield.
In broad daylight, yes, the hood of my car.

I scream, it goes away, just like that.
But if it comes back, what do I do?

HARVEY WALLBANGER

With a good old lousy Rita Hayworth Chinese
smuggling movie on, why do I watch tanker
spill news below the tail feathers of a stuffed

Schlitz peacock in this slump of a bar? Because
I like to take soundings of the bottomless muck
of the world. Because I like to pour another

shot to dump on my head for the jerk I have
backed myself into. Oh I wish people were
here so I could wish they would leave! Tell me

how wretched we are and I will match you low
for low, clink for clank. Am I ever going to come
in from the parking lot? They say you have to

hang your coat up before you can get yourself
a hallway to hang it in. They are probably right.
It's time to clean the feathers out of the car.

Peace to Harvey Wallbanger and everyone I've
dived by blindly crabbing, and peace to people
I will never meet being from around here only.

COLLATERAL DAMAGE

Bosnia, 1999

The bomb meant for a truck convoy
struck only a nursery. What a mess,
though, pieces of pots and plants
scattered everywhere. Another bomb

was meant for an ammo dump.
What an explosion that would have made!
When it struck the schoolhouse,
only a few children died. The other children

were hiding in cellars or had already died.
Then there was a ceasefire.
The mother went out to forage for food.
She left her son in charge of her baby.

Coming back, she dreamed, wide awake,
that dogs devoured her baby.
She dreamed it again, this time with rats.
She was already screaming when

she got back and grabbed up her baby.
Her son backed off. Other boys joked
that the dogs had not taken her kid
because it was too scrawny.

She tried to rip their windpipes from
their bodies. People pulled her away.
She went for the boys again
with her hands out like meat hooks.

AIR BALL

I'm shooting baskets on the driveway. I loft a soft
jumper: good arc, nice back-spin. It falls short, though,
touching nothing. Air ball. Hits the down spout, rolls

down the hill. Nuts. I go and get it and, dribbling back,
imagine the seconds ticking down—10, 9, 8—I must
pick my man off—7, 6, 5—finally daylight!—3, 2, 1—
my shot clangs off the rim. O.K., I try again—6, 5,

4, 3—I break clear, lift a long running onehander. In
and out. Refs reset the time clock: 5 seconds. I look
my defender in the eyes, go up over him. The shot

doesn't reach the rim. Air ball. One bounce, and the ball
is arcing out-of-bounds. I leap for it, teeter on the line.
The pricker bush won't hold me up. I sink, I hurt.
Whistle! I must've been pushed out. Refs are putting

seconds back on the clock. I pull prickers from my
shooting hand. After this time out, I'll be double-teamed.
That's O.K., they'll get me the ball, and there'll be time.

GREEN DIVER

A bright sky fell fast and dark into
the sea we had to flee the island
we scrambled to the shore and
pushed off in a small boat out
into choppy break we climbed
the face of the first few waves
got up over them but the next
waves were too big we had to try
to hold steady and let them break
over us then out beyond the break
the rowing seemed to go nowhere
as the trough from wave to wave
dropped deeper longer and darker
whatever you yelled I wouldn't
hear sit down sit down this dumb
thing done I'll do I'll row us out

and just as we were gaining
ground you fell overboard I
jumped in caught you sliding
deeper locked your shoulders
and kicked for air up through
the soupy green but we were
slapped back down every way
was water sand slashed our
faces you dug your face into
my chest the surf shoveled
us raked us across the pebble

bottom near shore I dragged
us onto the dry beach we
squeezed the hot sand
through our fingers and
squeezed it through again

WHEN I LISTEN IN MY CAR TO MOZART'S "DON GIOVANNI"

I usually cry at the same two places:
"Batti, batti, O bel Masetto"
and when they repeat *"Andiamo, bella campagna"*
or something like that.
I know *"andiamo"* means "let's go."
Which is O.K. if that's all you mean,
but *"andiamo,"* that's saying "let's go" with panache,
and who can't use a little panache?

I like singing lightly too
because then what I'm hearing
feels like me singing,
as if all I need to do is to sing lightly into the music
and the music becomes mine.

If I cry outright, I can't hear the music,
but if I sob, which is softer, I can
—I just can't sing.

I conduct myself too sometimes.
I steer with my left hand and conduct with my right.
I'm careful about passing cars.
I don't want people seeing me to think I'm, you know, off.

VALENTINE

with a nod to Donald Hall

Big frogs croak,
baby frogs slither;
I'd rather go broke
than not be with her.

Bull frogs croon,
slugs wiggle wider;
I'd live in ruin
to lie down beside her.

YOU'LL HAVE TO STAY FOR LUNCH AND THERE IS NO LUNCH

So why did I drag you over here when you're as boring
as all the other dead wood living along these hills?
My neighbor, that's why. Not a stir from him in weeks.
After all the good years of plastic rocket launchers.

And how about the bats he unleashed over here when
I hit fungoes onto his terrace? And the parties we threw
to make the other guy call the cops to break them up,
loud, lousy parties that cost a fortune. Listen up,

you go over there, say you're from a charity and you
want him to join the board because he's so upstanding.
He hates being called upstanding. If you don't go over,
you will have to stay for lunch and there is no lunch.

I can't believe you are related to him. You're so non.
Do you know what I mean: "non"? How could you?
He hasn't done something stupid, has he, like died?

NO PROBLEM

Look, if my neighbor says he heard screaming last night
coming from here, no problem, officer. I believe him.
Yes, I sit most of the day by this window that faces
his place. I can't help but see that things aren't
going well for him. I'm not going into it, no—and I wouldn't
respect anyone who did—but someone with lights
on all night, and that sound coming from his place.
Sure sounded like a scream to me. But hey,
what do I know? Like I said, I like the guy,
so I don't want to go into it. Just let me say, though:
you can go out of your head and hear screaming
from somewhere—but where?—
when it's really coming from you
and by the time you hear it, the scream is way out there.

WORRIED SICK IN KLAMATH FALLS

When the pelican comes in for its landing,
it leans back as if it's not sure.

The sand of the quarry hill may already be so hot
that the heat would come right through my shoes.

My daughter is too far away from me to understand
her fully the first time she tries to tell me.

Is she just being nice, sharing with her dad,
or is she afraid, and wants me to do something?

How does a pelican set up its landing
when the lake has such a sheen to it?

What is the fire that burns out the nightfall,
burns out the fear of a call about my daughter?

The ducks, landing on the lake, lean even farther back
as if they are going to change their minds.

Would the sand quarry hill give way, like a dune,
if I tried to climb it? What if I went on all fours?

My daughter speaks so fast I don't know if she is
trying to tell me something or trying not to.

Should I ask her to tell me again? Will she get mad?
Or am I just worrying because I want to?

The ducklings wobble along behind their parents.
Let's see, there are five. Is that fewer than before?

What is the fire that burns out the nightfall,
burns out the fear of the call about my daughter?

HOW DO YOU REALLY DO?

Mr. and Mrs. Very Big Deal step out onto our driveway
from the bank vault of their car,
rolling out hellos like tips.
My parents smile like little kids about to receive presents.
I stand there with them and try to push my tongue
up through the top of my mouth,
up at my brain.
Then I squeal without letting any of the squeal out.

I know them again, Mr. and Mrs. Very Big Deal,
by the way they shake my hand
that shakes slightly expecting her drooped
stem of a hand to sleep in my hand,
while his grip barks from the hip
as he gives me my name like a promotion,
peels it off like dollar bills from a wad,
that weird vegetable of money,
and free to me, only me.
He knows, he just knows, he is my congratulations.

I am tempted to tell them that I paint tiny bombs
to look like birds' eggs
and climb to the nest on the pole
at the amusement park and place the eggs
in the nest of the gray hawk that sees for miles.
But I won't tell,
they wouldn't get it anyway
and I'd get in trouble with my parents.

I try to forget that I'm letting myself down.
I push my tongue up again at the top of my mouth.
Then I squeal without letting any of the squeal out.

GOOD MORNING COFFEE MAKES FOR A BUZZ

These people around me at this coffee shop,
they are not from here. I've never seen
them before, but, in all fairness, they don't
seem to be trying to take over. True, around
the Half and Half, they are pretty pushy,
and no human should be content to look
so unkempt. Surely they've heard of a comb.

Who knows, limited funds may have cut back
their human imitation training. Their clothes,
who on earth would wear them? The tall
creature with the singing shoes, he should
wear a hat like that only if he is stone bald.
But for an old white guy, he moves with
the glint of a dancer. And who says you have

to look sharp to appreciate good coffee?
What are they doing now tapping those long
walking sticks together and swaying in unison?
But here is the point: if you looked into this
coffee shop right now, would you notice me?
I doubt it. Keeping a low profile is a must
in this work. Move little, stay nonchalant,

take no notes, and focus, focus. Do these
vegetable creatures pose a threat to our
planet's security? Not for me to decide,
I'm just a volunteer in the field. "I'll see

you guys tomorrow," I say as I mosey out.
Maybe tomorrow I'll get the nerve up to ask
the tall guy where he got the singing shoes.

WHAT GRANDFATHER DID AT HIS FUNERAL

People at his funeral said grandfather rose up in his coffin,
looked around, and slammed the coffin lid back down.
When I got home and told my family,
they said, "You're just a crazy little kid."
But people were afraid of grandfather,
said he could come back as one of those big black
squawking birds if we didn't get him good right now.

I hadn't thought about his funeral until today, years later.
These people, a bunch of nose hairs, dressed me
in this suit that's too tight, tried to plaster my hair down,
and started lowering me in this casket
into a grave. It feels like your bed is going down
through the floor and you can't wake up.

Now they start to pull me back up out of the grave,
and what I am thinking about
is that the river is wearing away this hill
and one of these days the river will lift the cemetery
and float it off, and maybe grandfather and I
will float down the hill, too, sitting up in our open caskets.

The town will be flooding. We will save a couple of dogs
and dock at a magistrate's house, tie up our caskets
to his porch railing, introduce ourselves,
suggest that he break out his Silver Fox,
the renowned vodka of our region,
and call for some scraps for the shivering dog.

WHEN THE RED WIND BLOWS

Where do we go when we finally go?
Does go mean gone? Or is gone a flow
that goes on forever? What does it mean
if there's above and below? Can you tell,
before, which way you're headed?
O dear in the dark I don't want to know.

What about Mom: What about Dad?
What about our dog buried out back?
Some nights his ghost plays on his bones
like on a xylophone. I can't sleep.
At school I fall asleep. My teachers,
why can't they leave me alone,
let me sit on my shadow

on the bank of a brook? I promise, I won't
shoot birds, I won't light bugs on fire.
But what if I have to go to war
and I'm the ball turret gunner on a B-17?
Will I blubber into my oxygen mask?
Will I sight in steady on enemy planes
or freeze in my head and pee in my pants?

Mom and Dad, they say that when the right
time comes, they'll be ready to go.
How do they know? They could be hit tomorrow
by a car or fall down a hole. I bet they tell us
all this so we'll sleep through the night
when the red wind blows.

TAKING ON A GOON OF DEATH

This spindly guy with a watery left eye
and bad teeth, like he just had a big spinach salad,
introduces himself as a beachcomber
when each woman around the beach party fire
picks a guy for the horse fights. "I'll take the new guy,"
I say into a swarm of snickers,
but I know bad when I see bad, and I really want to win.

Look at this guy; open overcoat, sunken chest
sporting four long white hairs and splotched Man Tan.
And that smile, like a rusty razor blade.
I climb up on his shoulders, get a good grip
from the back on a woman's hair,
and knee my guy in the ribs. He pulls,
over they go. Whoopee! We wipe team after team

through the fire pit. His scalp smells like phlegm.
So what, we're winning. Whoops, he runs off with me
down the hard wet sand. I'm in trouble,
got to con him. I coo, slush a kiss,
tickle his arm pits. Nobody,
not even a goon of death, is taking me down,
not now, not here. I lean over and whisper

in his left ear, "Why don't we switch
and I'll give you a good piggyback."
He gurgles, gives in. I get the goon up on my back,
whisk him into the ocean, and dump him.

His overcoat fills like a sandbag. I dunk him once,
twice, hold him under until all that comes up
is yellow fizz like sarsaparilla.

IT'S SHIFTS OF SIDEWAYS IF SHE TALKS TO YOU

For the teenager certain she is fat, it's shifts
of sideways if she talks to you. Words
drop out. She tries to get behind herself

and squeeze down
to a gash in the ground.
Oh she would love to roll from her skin

and disgust you. Stick it to your candy pity, yeah.
She takes a deep breath
and throws her hair around like rocks.

THE FOAM MACHINE

What if you were a fire burning out a house?
You can't last forever, you know it, but for now
you're better than all the shouts, sirens, and water
they can throw at you.
Heck, they can line up the engines
and try to drown you in a broadside, but they can't touch
your lick and laugh.
You steam the water into a skin
and work yourself up for a higher leap.
Who knows, you might reach a star
and blaze away happy
—when up skids another firetruck
and two firemen lift off a big metal box with a hose
the size of a sewer pipe.
You're going to broil it and spit out the metal pieces.
Oh how you love the smell of burning rubber!
Go ahead, you guys, jam that box on the front door
like a toilet plunger.
You're all over it,
but it won't burn. The hose foams,
the front room foams. it eats your air. You flash,
stagger, rush for the walls. A lather coating
cuts you off. You lick away
to another room. You're not up
to making a run for it,
and if you try to fatten up, it will find you, you know it.
So it's huddle in a corner.
Foam feels you out and feeds.

MY LONELINESS

My loneliness never gets enough attention
from me. If I got a dog or cat, I hate to think
what it would do. I gave up on having our book
club meet here. The worst time is Christmas.
It believes in Santa Claus and wants me to take
it to the mall to sit on Santa's lap. "You've got
to be kidding! You're my age! What do you think,
you can roll me around like some old tire?"

A woman I was ga-ga about, who put up with
all this, saying it was "a challenge," told me
to set food in a bowl outside my apartment
and push my loneliness out the door. I did.
When it got back in, it convinced her
I should be more caring. Weeks after she left,
I was still re-arranging furniture, and going
to one sad yard sale after another.

One minute I feel like a scramble of hair
from my hair brush, the next minute like
much too much butter on my bread. I try
to act as if I don't have a big loneliness.
But what if someone finds him? I could say
"Oh yeah, you mean my old Big Foot costume."
Pretty good, huh? But all the time I'll know
my loneliness is mine, it's me, it's family.

THE LAST PLACE IN TOWN TO STOP SMOKING

The joint was to be shut down
for refusing to prohibit smoking. People vied,
on both sides, to be more indignant.
And the lost souls living up over the place,
they would have to leave. They didn't bother anyone,
except during parades. Dashed from the sidewalk
into the parade and kissed people.

Days before eviction,
an emphysema institute in the next state
bought the place for a song
and bussed in their smokers, guys who cough like crazy,
women too—cough as if
they were going to blow their guts out;
and the minute they stop light up another cigarette.
They look like clay people.
They look like people waiting a long time for a bus
and trying to decide it's not coming.

As for the institute, it's pretty much left alone now.
Some people go out there.
The cafeteria, open to the public, is a good place,
visitors say, to sit and think about stopping smoking.
Maybe even talk about quitting.
Now and then, perhaps because they get excited,
someone lights up.

THE LITTLE TREES ARE OLDER THAN I AM

My grandparents' room looked out over the little trees
I am standing by. Theirs was the best room in the house,
with moldings shiny like a fish
and windows big as adults. I used to stand
in the center of the room and look out over the little trees.
Only a couple of weeks had passed
since my grandparents' funerals
when I saw my grandparents out the window,
waving at me from the trees.
I waved back. I remember thinking,
what if I climb into the tops of the little trees?

I climbed out the window, the trees swayed to the ground,
and back up. I hung on,
then walked away, dizzy as a weed.
I could have killed myself.
Kids do things like this,
like for a game to see if you can kill yourself,
then make the game into a joke.
Some kids believe they cannot die as long as
they are pretending.
They say this, they don't really believe it, though.
I know I can die. I've seen my blood
spread into the bathtub water like red smoke.

DOWN ON ALL FOURS

Sometimes, when I'm alone, someone talks to me.
"Who are you?" I ask.
They stop talking. I do too,
but I'm lonely and I don't realize I'm talking.

When I was young, I could slip down into myself
like when I got depressed or scared,
and pull myself back up.
It was kind of fun.

But now I can get dizzy,
black out, and fall down. I get scared,
so I start talking to make sure I'm alive,
down on all fours, staring at the floor,
waiting for things to clear.
My cat scolds me. Keep talking, cat.
I'm ashamed. It's like I'm doing something stupid
and can't help it.

What if one of my children drops by
and finds me like this? And if I'm talking to no one,
I can say goodbye to this house and cat.

CLOUDS ROLL OVER THE MOUNTAINS
LIKE SO MANY LITTLE HILLS

When I sit in the silence of late afternoon,
the sky looks like the light of someone's life.
Depressing. So I think of the four of us old folks
sitting out here on the porch,
pretending the sun warms us as it warms the porch stones,
but we are cold, always cold.
The nurses get us up and walk us around.
Shuffle, shuffle, boil, and puffle.
I wonder if we even look much like people,
more like little dead trees.
Let's say the sun slides behind the mountain
or plows into a cloud, then the cold drops in fast,
but who cares, the sky is beautiful. Banks of clouds
bask in the bright, full, fall light.
Hey, I like to say to the others,
look at the clouds roll over the mountains
like so many little hills!
They aren't listening.
They say they are making their peace.
What do you take me for?
Don't yell, they say. They will hear you in the lobby
and take our privileges away.
Oh, just look at their new sneakers,
the goody-goody white and their blue blue hair.
Now that's depressing.
Here's what I think I'll do: smack them.

Not hard, but hard enough to bring them around.
Then lift them out of their chairs
and dance them around.
So maybe they dance like brooms, so what.

I'M ON A SMALL LEDGE BELOW A PEAK

I'm on a small ledge below a peak
while the mountain slides slowly away.
Or is it clouds lifting that makes me feel
we are sliding down?
I stand up, I sit back down.
If we'd only stay in one place.
Another mountain peak rises nearby
through the clouds it seems.
My ledge drops even with the peak
and further down into a cloud.
The air inside smells like vegetables.
I'm cold. My small ledge
slides out into open air.
Maybe I will be all right after all.
I'll concentrate on my grandchildren.
I imagine them opening
their glass jars, squealing
as the yellow butterflies fly away,
and with their hands in the air,
running after the butterflies.
I wave to them. They don't see me.
Perhaps this is the way it should be.

MY TIME MAY COME ANY TIME

I'm feeling a little flimsy this morning.
Maybe the nurses shouldn't have let me out for a walk.
I need to look down.
That's no fun.
I'm an old shack that stays up by leaning into itself.
That's no fun either. But I like to walk this path
and watch the sunlight flicker on the water.
I stop, the sunlight
goes still on the water. Keep going, you goat.
If you stop to rest, you'll doze off and get cold.
My time could come any time.
I talk with my friends about this.
I like what they say about your time coming.
There is a train, they say,
and if it stops for you
then you have to board.
Here's what they say about baggage:
you may carry a bag but you can't have anything in it.
The bag is not for looks,
it's to hold on to.

from *The Brink* (2000)

SNOW AT NIGHT

I am so far away
that from there I can hear myself talking to someone
and an echo like when you turn away from a river
and you can't tell
if it's the river right then
or a sound of the river echoing through you.

I want to go there and watch in the eddies near the shore.
The caught sticks turning, then popping back,
then turning again,
as if they would break in two to shake free.

I'm like the snow at night in the field.
Most of the time you can't see it, then it glistens.

BIRDS THAT BEAT THE SKY TO BITS

The old biddy was a fool, but when she went,
she left a hole big enough to fall in.
The old coot next door isn't much better,
about as much fun as old bread. Always out
clipping his bushes, and when I went by,
he nodded, tipped his hat. When he looks up now,
into the mirror, he doesn't know sometimes
he is there. That's the stroke. One minute
you're someone, the next you're not.

He doesn't come out anymore. If he wanted to,
and stand by his bushes, I would stand
with him. If he got to feeling pretty good,
I would take him to where the birds
settle in the flyway, and be there
for the first time they all lift.
Oh my, the screeching and flapping
as they beat the sky to bits!
I'll say "migration." Maybe he will too.
I'll say "migration, my gracious!" It's fun.
He may get a laugh out of that. We can laugh,
you know, even when we are pretty shot.

I MIGHT BREAK, I MIGHT DISAPPEAR

I am standing in the doorway in my snowsuit.
I love my snowsuit, I want to wear it all the time.
I am so excited that I see someone,
probably myself, across the field,
emerging from the falling snow.
I don't move for fear the person won't come,
or will come and will leave me. I know,
I am just standing there, but I am afraid
I might break, I might disappear,
or not be able to speak when I speak.
It's the snow. It piles
and piles, yet nothing falls over.
The first time I saw snow
I was looking up and up
at white coming down everywhere,
and mother looking down at me
was saying snow.
She meant white landing on my face
and hands was snow. Snow she said again
and caught it on her tongue. She meant taste too!
I caught snow on my tongue. I even said it.
And best of all, I heard myself say snow, snow.

STANDING WATER

It used to be I could turn in my chair
because moments came up like trains
and passed as easily as fields
passed me sitting on a train.
But no longer. My inner ear hums.
Things go a little off, like water standing
where water shouldn't be.
I put my hand down here,
and here is over there.
Crossing a room, I stop by a table
and can't stop. Sometimes
when I stop by a table,
I am not there yet.
Now and then, the boards on the floor
tip a little and I tip a little and, angling,
have to brace myself for the wall.
I go along it with my hands.
It's like they are walking along the wall.
Windows I don't enjoy much.
I look out but my mind won't go out.
Windows make me look back at myself.

BAD DAY

Don't assume I am writing anything down,
or plan to, or that I can stand reading it,
even when there is nothing to do, or that
I have any idea of what I am going to write;
and don't think for a minute it's any fun.
It's not. These are dumb notions I won't
explain, except they run around like cats
and writing is the only way to trap them, rid
them. It beats biting my lips to bits. Crazy?
There is not enough left of me to go crazy.
People old as me don't go crazy. We dribble
away, a part at a time, and the live parts,
they are too dumb to know what else to do,
even when the part next to them breaks.
Don't come after these papers either. They
go with with me, stuffed into my clothes, see.
When the clothes shrivel and blow open,
the papers float into the nothing they talk to.

GLINT

You see the chair out there in the field?
I love it. And the two big stones?
They are so smooth they could have
rolled in the ocean for years. This was once
an ocean floor. I like to imagine that.
The two big stones, I call them sun stones.
They send sunlight out and out across the valley.
I imagine my words going out there too,
when I speak. So I think hard
about what I am going to say. The stream passing
in front of me, I watch it and pretend
the words form in the stream.
The stream helps me think.
The stream helps me not to think, too. To get here,
the stream comes miles across the valley,
down from the mountains, snowcapped year round,
mountains you see only now and then
as if, through the night, they pull away again.
I would like to move like the mountains
and move like the stream, too.
Even in a mist, the stream has a glint to it.

BLUE BLUE HAIR

I am on the floor, on my back. I must have fallen,
knocked myself cuckoo. Oblong, everything
is oblong. My mouth tastes bad. Some of it I think
got turned inside out when I fell. The rug
smells of ammonia. I hum my slow song about almonds
to soothe me. Down here, I can lick my own blood.
As a kid, I could wrap a hose around a tree,
then turn the water on hard, make that hose
jump like a snake. Not anymore.
If only I could hear a good banjo,
I'd lie here until I was cold liver.
As long as that bridge group of mine
doesn't find out. They would like nothing better
than to get something on me and razz me
until I break out. Sure, I put silverware
in their coat pockets and try to be there
when they pull it out. You can see the idea
cross their faces, slow as a bug,
as if that blue blue hair dulls the brain.

I WON'T NEED LEGS THERE

I weigh less than some dogs,
and where I am going I want to be smaller still,
especially my head, thick and sagging.
I won't need legs there.
My hands, poor things,
more and more like bird wings.
I hide them. I have started to go—
when I turn in my chair and wave to someone leaving,
the person isn't leaving, I am.
I think of waving
but the air doesn't work
and I'm smaller, lighter, and passing through.

DO NOT LET THEM TAKE ME AWAY IF NAKED

Do not let them take me away if naked
they find me out on the lawn with the Purple Martins
swooping around their birdhouses
and me pretending the Purple Martins listen
when I speak. I say that to pass the time;
I don't know when I will die.
Besides, the night grass is wet and cold.

Do not let them take me away if naked
they find me down on the dock,
or leaning against a piling and facing out
over the water, or in a rowboat tied to the dock,
on the floorboards, leaning back
with my head on the seat in the stern
and getting dizzy from the stars.

Do not let them take me away if naked
they find me cast off from the dock, floating
around the pond, under what we have for clouds
and a moon. I am ninety-six. Who is to say
I won't know when my times comes;
and I don't want any clothes getting in the way.
That would be like leaving in a sack.

FULL HEAT THAT FLUTTERS

I spread the fingers on my hand and stare through the spaces.
I like time with little in it,
like a puddle, something but with little in it.
I am getting smaller, and I'm trying to keep growing too,
in here, in my heart. This means I must make room
in my heart. Must move people on, years and years of people.
Friends grow roots thick as rope.
Friends cling, they die and don't let go.
Ivy on the woodpile and the trunks of trees, I cut it
but it won't come off.
It's like my friends. I have to rip it off.
I tell friends I love them but I don't want to see them
all the time. They pout
like their cats. And worse, they let their worries
squeeze them into twigs.
I call these "the frights." They're like boils:
rub them and they get worse.
I don't want to go in my sleep.
I like the porch. I'll pull my chair along to hold the shade.
I want light, high morning light, and a breeze.
And heat, full heat that flutters.

COMING HOME

Sometimes I need to be there for a while
before I can really be there, as if I need to
sneak up on returning home to you
—say, park down street and, coming up to the house,

set my hand in the mailbox,
say, palm down, to see if I left
a message, and think what
the message might be, between the mailbox and the house;

draw my fingers along the ridges of the mailbox,
and think about messages
sliding along the ridges,
sliding in and out under the ceiling,

the nicely arched ceiling of the mailbox,
and, before leaving, lift the flap that hangs, when
open, like a tongue;
lift the mailbox flap gently enough

not to disturb the space
you like me to reach for you through,
that you enjoy your own sifting through
—a space you float to allow us both

our own leaning in and leaning out,
a kind of transparent balloon
we can move toward one
another within. I'm already

at the front door, feeling the key
find the keyhole; and quickly
I'm between the door opening
and hearing you coming toward me,

between your continuing to appear
more clearly and your arms opening. I slip
my arms under your arms, lift
you and, for a long deep breath, hold you aloft.

HALLOWEEN OF THE SUDDEN HAND

We wait for dark, then, dressed commando,
move as one, like cilia. We work backyards and sheds,
hanging heads we made from junk and painted loony
in my cellar. Once little kids scarf the candy
and front porch lights go off, we stalk
the shadow side of the pointed-turret house
where the old crazy lady lives with her retarded son.
We creep our pole up to a lit window on the second floor
and tap our brown-paper head with green marbles for eyes.
No luck. Gently we lift it over to the next window,
a dark window. A hand comes out,
pats our head and takes out one eye. After that,
anyone messing with the old lady answers to us.

A MAN ON A BICYCLE

If I squint just right into the sun
and the handlebars don't jiggle,
I see double stacks of hay bales
as ziggurats. They hold the field
like temples, and Queen Anne's Lace
lines the roadside ditches.
Around ten at night, quail sound
their mating call, which gives me
the willies, like when a peacock
stared into the side mirror
of a pickup truck, dangling upside down,
the mirror that is. In lovemaking,
there is the nimble, twang, and vichyssoise
and how your bones become bamboo
in the slow scattering of feathers around them.

TRAFFIC JAM ON THE ROSS ISLAND BRIDGE

for Dennis Meiners

I am knuckled in here on the Ross Island Bridge,
heading west, toward the West Hills of Portland.
The hills are ridged by trees in silhouette
against the sunset. Strands of clouds loll over the trees,
sink into them, and snag. One strand settles in the trees
like a big, gray nest. If there is no Northwest bird
that lays its eggs in such a nest, inventing it is my job.
My potter friend and I will envision the bird.
I will tell my friend that white sunset
comes down on the nest and shimmers it;
and darkness, thick with rain, pushes the light
down into the trees. There is not enough sky for rain
to get down easily. The rain is slowed by rain
below it. Why hurry? This is Oregon, rain is lazy here.
Wind shoots rain up in sheets that topple back
and fall through themselves. Between the tree line and
the darkness falling are planes of light,
measuring miles across. Rain does not faze them.
These slabs slide through themselves,
across the entire city. I'd love to have one hover
over my backyard some early evening,
and take friends out to toast it.

NIGHT FISHING

The water is a glaze like loneliness at ease
with itself. I cast and close my eyes for the whir
out across the water, the line striking the surface
and sinking. I like waiting for it to settle on the bottom,
then jig it up a little. I imagine the lure in utter dark.
I play it lightly. Fish rise. Just shy of the surface,
they play their glints off the moon on the water.
I see too my own loneliness. It's not too big
and it breathes easily. Soon, it may pretend it's rain.
Rain blurs the water. There is nothing wrong
with rain. I take a deep breath and cast and cast.

SOME OF THE DEAD GO TO THE CITY

Some of the dead go to the city. They can hide there,
they don't have to talk. They can't. They love
to sit out on front porches. All the cars and busses
and neon signs and people on the sidewalk
and people crossing the street
and yelling. City people talk to themselves a lot,
talk to all the people they are at once.
The dead love this. They nod and shuffle their hands.
The dead have trouble, though, keeping their heads up
and their mouths from sagging open,
so they lean their heads against a wall,
and hold their mouths closed. Attention they don't like,
especially from the little kids who point and talk loud.
Even in summer, the dead wear overcoats, like drunks.
They can stare you down, scare you away,
but you might tell someone, and they don't move fast.
They hate trying, they hate to do much of anything
but sit on the front porch when it's not too hot,
traffic is snarled and radios are blaring.

THE BRINK

This chair and window and day, dear things
crowding me crazy—me, Mr. hi ho here
and ho hum blow your nose over there. I don't care,
anything to keep the old memory rash from heating up.
I can't help fiddling with it. I sweat. I guess
I scratch some scabs off and dizzy out,
woozy as a weed. When I land a reason to go out,
the reason caves in at the door as if it were kidding.
I lie back down and listen to the rain plink plonk
the broken gutter puddle. I make the sound, too.
With each drip, I pop my lips. And do some humming.
I should take the garbage out, I know that.
My chest has a drummer in it who is a showoff.
I can settle if I don't look at the phone.
Wads of phlegm break up on their own.
I pretend I am on a long train that sleeps by day.
At night I float, tiny, from one page of a comic book
to the next. I put words in the ovals.
A good little thriller can come out of this.
Time for sit ups. Look at those toes, the little rabbits!
I am a moving van, empty, doors ajar, with a stack
of tarps in the corner behind the driver.
Here is the plan: I will take one room of the house
at a time and quietly. When the racket comes,
I never cook. Never make salads. No knives.
I sit on my hands. The racket comes at night, too,
when I'm asleep; I'm yelling before I know

what I am saying. The same racket I try to
wash out when I shower over and over again,
that I eat out when I eat and don't eat.

WHAT SCARED ME AS A BOY WAS NOT MY SEX

What scared me as a boy was not my sex,
my father, or the world, but how calmly
I joined others in taking a creature apart,
like a cat over its stunned prey,

looking away, smacking it from time to time,
and the thick quiet, the prolonging,
the same quiet as in my dream
of staring out across the huge fish I stand on,

shoving my hands into air holes
on the fish's back and making spouts.
I bring a deck chair up on its back,
stick in an umbrella and, at night,

make little fires. The fish doesn't cry out,
doesn't even move. I think it wants me there,
down through its dying. Or is it giving birth
and taking care of the child will be my job?

VICTIM

He came at her, enraged. She froze,
just as she had the last time.
In the hospital, when she was again conscious,
he slobbered promises until she forgave him.
She dreamed of fish,
little fish that chanced by her sea cave
and she closed her eyes as she closed her jaws
over them. She didn't leave her cave
for fear her swimming would drive light
through her body and creatures would mock
and nibble her until she was helpless.

As he came at her, enraged, again, she felt herself
shrinking. She became too small to finish
the laundry, too small to get the children
off to school. She needed time to think
before he beat her. She stepped aside.
He stumbled past her, fell,
and came at her again.
She was thinking of wet laundry
and the children, who had already missed
so much school. She jumped aside.
He thrashed past her, turned, and charged.
She brought her knee up into his groin
and scratched his face. He went over.
She fell on him, bit him,
buried her mouth in his neck
until people, yelling, pulled her off.

From time to time now,
she turns her hands over and over,
looking, she says, for things that crawl
from under her blouse onto her wrists.

BIG SHOT GRACES THE OLD BAR & GRILL

What you say? What you crazy?
It's me, I'm back! Hey, ugly,
here's looking at you. You guys,
the old gang, Barflies. Barflies.

Maybe I buy this place as a tax deduction,
list you deadbeats as a bunch of luncheons.
Ha! Not bad, huh? If you want
to smile, get some teeth. Doesn't

anyone do anything here? Lift the blinds!
When a guy comes home, it's high time
he's deserving. If anyone got out of here,
remember what we promised? Sure,

we wrote in blood: we'd throw a party
for him. You just didn't figure on me,
right? No, not the little fat kid
you beat up all the time. You did,

admit it. Now's your chance.
Hey, don't all talk at once.
That's a joke. I'm kidding.
O.K., I'm not kidding.

You're an old debt
I've come to collect
on. Probably you
haven't a clue

what I'm saying.
So listen, I'm paying.
Drinks are on me.
This party for you is for me.

THE DISTANCE

You lean down close enough to blow me over
and say, "don't need anything you can't
buy, take or, with your own hands, make.
Do that and you'll be like me. That's
what you want. You want to be my son."

And when you left, you left your distance
for me to feed on. Stuff came up. "Spit
it out, boy; so people deserve our trust,
huh? Grow up, assume the worst."

I didn't know your tough-guy talk was smoke
to cover up your dry martini heart. You took
your disappointment out on me, a kid,
and my kid brother. That's gutless,
I'd love to crack your distance now across

your grave. Just what you'd like: I'd prove
you right, I'd never get away. So here, I give
you back your distance, all I've dislodged,
year by year, chunk by rancid
chunk. A little boy can take a lot.

THEY CAME HERE TO DIE

They came here to die, the elegant young men
at the café across the street
in the full sun of this Sunday afternoon in San Francisco.
A row of tables lines the sidewalk,
and behind them, against the wall, the young men
have placed all the chairs, facing out.
They lean back in the chairs against the building
and gaze across the street,
across the square behind me,
for all I know across their whole journey here
to this day, to this café in San Francisco.
They don't talk. They don't look at me either.
Probably, they pretty much despise me for staring at them,
or they don't care.
I suppose, if I learned I was dying,
I would leave people I knew
to be with people who understand.
I could join my dying to their dying.
Nobody could tell me to disappear.

from *Tour* (1987) & *I Want to Be a Crowd* (1979)

DEAR MR. SEARS,

I want to write you about your poem about the frog.
I love frogs. I raised one once. My mother made me
stop kissing it. I like your poem.

> Yours sincerely,
> Mrs. X

Dear Mrs. X,

Thank you. Writers appreciate a personal response—
what else is there? What is it like in Brule, Nebraska? And
where did you see the poem? I don't recall it. Really.
Which makes me feel pretty silly. Please sign your
name. It's good of your to write.

> Yours truly,
> Peter Sears

Dear Mr. Sears,

It must be strange not to recall the poem. That's all
right. Here are the last two lines, my favorites—

> I roll the frog over on its back
> and tickle him under his little chin sack.

> Sincerely yours,
> Mrs. X

Dear Person,

I can see why you like the poem, but I didn't think
frogs stayed put that long. Anyway, I can't take credit
for the poem. And yes, it is strange.

> Yours,
> Peter Sears

Dear Peter Sears,

The poem is 'My Friend the Frog' published in the third grade paper. The rest of the poem is blurred by dirt and leaves.

Yours,
a friend

BIKE RUN

Old summers would begin
wearing down the path again, the bike run
that slit the hip-high field into long triangles.

Hit the start hard and standing, jump
the rock gap, the gully, feet up
for puddles in the middle.

Slick along the packed sand
and streak out the other end
leaning on the sky,

And the breathless one inside you,
who wants to sleep in high grass,
tell him there is a path through,

That you made the path through.
Show him, tell him again;
make him shout, I believe you.

GRANDFATHER AND THE RABBIT

Upstate, in a town with brown benches
and stores with houses on top of them,
we stopped the car along a high stone sidewalk
and father led us to Grandfather's church,
planks, thick with paint, a bird's nest
by the door, official man in the door.
He leaned a little like a tree
and smiled so fast his eye blinked.

The church went straight to the altar.
Rows went out like bones of big wings.
I felt the organ playing through the floor,
like the towns, driving up,
getting lower and farther away.

Most towns up here went away years ago,
father said, when the textile mills
moved south. I didn't understand. I thought
Grandfather died softly like snow.

Father spun the wheel
to miss a rabbit crushed on the road.
He tried to blend his swerve into a turn,
and mother mentioned flowers and how well
they plow the roads up here. Lines
in her face were trees across a cloud.
I puffed up my window and drew eyes.

I know how rabbits die on roads
but Grandfather in this place,
what happened to his thud step?
It's out there. I want to be out there.

We were standing in the pew. I stepped on
my shined shoes. Mother gave me her hand.
I let it go away.

TO A YOUNG WOMAN CONSIDERING SUICIDE

When everything you touch you've already touched,
you can't sleep, can't eat, can't even
remember when you could, you go on living;

When everywhere you are you want to leave,
it's so stupid, stupid not to go down
with the sun, down with leaves spiraling,

Down with the duck pulled under
by the muskrat, waves, they don't roll in,
they roll down and die—even now, you go on living.

Would you help me with my plant?
See, it's not doing well at all, and out
there in the snow my friend's car is stuck.

He needs a hand, what do you think?–
More light? A bigger pot? And what do I say
to my child, to your child someday,
if she goes out, as you have, under the long shadow?

MOON GLIDING

Woody Creek Canyon, Colorado

A raft down the river in the moon,
moon gliding, that's what we do
when the moon climbs the bank trees
and takes the river. The raft
goes in cold, slick, and slow off
from shore until the moon quickens
on the current. Banks, trees sink
back and blur. Water rollicks
in shallow rock beds. White water
is fast but moon water is slippery.
Glide, glide. Lifts of light tell
of boulders underwater, and over
smooth exposed stones water slides
so thin the moon goes right inside.

THE LADY WHO GOT ME TO SAY SOLONG MOM

Somewhere along the lettuce I nudge a lady who says
Amazing how you resemble my daughter! At the yogurt
we meet again. Would you say Solong Mom for an old
woman who misses her daughter? . . . Why not, for a lady
daffy in loneliness, Solong Mom. I end up behind her
at the checkout line. the guy rings up my lettuce,
yogurt and yam and says $43.16 . . . What! You're nuts!
. . . Your mother says the checkbook's in your purse.

My mother! She's not my mother. Out the door I shoot,
scan the parking lot. She's loading up the back seat,
the front seat. Hey, get back in and pay! She hips me,
we grapple. She's strong, then she's sad and weak,
standing there, staring around. The cart rolls off,
a bag dumps. We grab at each other. This is crazy.
She tilts her head, I tilt mine. Smack! She gets me
one good. I clout her. Get back in there and pay!

Whoopee! She yelps and gallops around me whoopeeing,
swinging her purse, and pops me on the nose. I tackle
her, grab a skinny leg, drag her across the lot like
an old hose, through the whooshing door, squiggling,
kicking. The manager hollers, What's going on? . . .
This lady just tried to rob me by pretending she's
my mother. That's right. Ask the checkout guy, $43.16
for my lettuce, yogurt and yam . . . Is that true, ma'am?

I don't have a daughter, I don't have a son. Cats
and a parakeet named Oswald who's deaf. He loves
the three-way light bulbs I lift from Woolworth's.
My old kook roommate babbles about being a princess.
It's enough to make you want to flush your head. This
girl is the daughter I really want. I want to ask her
back for dinner. I feel a lot better now. Thanks.

THE MOONLIGHT IS DEEP AND LONG

after a poem by William Carlos Williams

We have stayed out too long and still
we haven't picked enough fruit.
Our parents, we'll catch hell;
but if we can pick enough,
maybe they will let us out
tomorrow night. Let's bring back
baskets of pears! The heat, I said,
is why I lagged behind today.
Anyway, stars are easier
than all those people.
Your eyes shine so. The wind
is cool enough to walk with.
Look at this basket of pears,
cool skins of the moon's attention.
Baskets and baskets of pears!
Look at you in the moonlight.

BROTHER

You are only two years into your city.
Come back to nights when wind paws trees
and we have to talk to fall asleep.
Back into late afternoons
when the light strokes the gray pond
and the sun rocks long-haired in the reeds.

We ease in, sputtering the chill.
The sandy bottom loosens, comes smoking
to the surface, and we're under and rolling
in colors sliding like oil on water.

How still we float to let the wind
fall asleep on the pond,
then wake the wind, feel it brush
our backs like short fur. Tell me what burns
when the wind breaks in on the sun,
there, where the reeds lean away.

ESCAPE FROM EAST BERLIN

The Berlin Wall went through our heads.
Fed by day, by our staying in the East,
we drank it out at night. Our heads got
soft as beer. We toasted our escape plan,
the only place the Vopos hadn't walled,
where the river widens and searchlights
swing like waltzers. A guard could fire
and load again. A man could have a smoke.
This worst chance made our chances fair.

We swam the river and won't leave this bank.
Others will hear how we went and wonder
why not and plan. Before they can move,
police will hear and alert the authorities,
who will alert the border guards, and they
will alert the river, the dogs, the night.
There in the high grass on the east side,
is that a rock that tries to be the moon?
A face? A searchlight rolls the grass.

Stay down. Flush your stomach to the grass.
Count the black time between each beam.
Your heart jacks up the count. The brain
blows black and yellow. Count it hard
again. You've got to bet. Go, push off
from the cold sand lip. Hold your kick
until you're under; then kick, pull down
through the dark. Don't nick the top
until the beat is nailing down your throat.

FOGBANK

I am Fogbank. Born casual and drifty
I added leaping hedges and grinning,
if caught, with an electric face.
Why talk when you can stay gray
as your name? Rise, Fogbank, shuffle

The school steps, the job steps, loft
your dream flesh over mobile homes,
perch on the treeline of a deep estate,
soothe girls iceteaing on the terrace,
bored as cardboard, eager as pebbles
in the brook. Stretch out in the brook,

Dangle while the mother of all money
and things with names affirms: "I wish
more young men could act this way."
I know who to thank, but save it until
after dinner, when brandy has my tongue.

Old Whiffleball, I'm heading upwind,
frisky and shadowboxing. I am my own
prune's pit. I've never had an arm die
or an eye, nothing that tests the grain.
I've pickled long enough. Step into the
nightmare knucklers, the breaking stuff.

I'LL GIVE YOU FALL AND WINTER

Why didn't you stay in the windy fall
where you left me
to flap around my hard house?

Why didn't you stay in the dense winter
where you held me
tight as ice against my memory of you?

And spring too, why? Spring's
not like you. Buds, what can I do
against what they lift in me?

OPENERS

So you want to go up to someone and say
Scappoose! and you'd like to go over
to anyone and bow and bow and rising say
Nehalem. Please don't. Make up as many

openers as you want, as many as the
years passing over oceans, but don't
say them. It's foolish. That's OK
but it's helpless. Really. Sorry.

Scappoose! See? What's someone to say?
Nothing. Except Scappoose back.
Then what? See what I mean?
So you want to go up to someone

and right on by, keeping the lid on
What do you think is an original pet?
or, Will we be known centuries from now
as the people with hair? See how silly

it is? You're laughing! That proves it.
So just Scappoose yourself and have
a good laugh. Let those tears
swamp your nose. Just like that, yes.

Come on, you old Scappoose, hold on
to me. Good. Now let's bow. You can
do it. Nehalem. Off the second bow.
Nehalem. Good. Again. Nehalem.

IT'S IN THE EYES

What do cannibals do first when they catch you?
Lick. They want to know what to expect. Now
if they back off, surprise them: offer one
a lick. Stare. Tempt him to doubt his tongue.
Eyeball one goon over to you and with scorn
blistering indicate to him that the water has
been left unattended.—Stoke it, stoke it,
you toady! And wood, get wood!—Shame them
and when they get pots, utensils, condiments
and their breast beating statues, take charge.

The ones gathering straw, kick their butts,
lick at them, laugh.—More straw, boobies!
Decadent, you guys are decadent. Hell, you've
got no taste.—Next, the tasty combinations
gambit. Grab yams, line them along your leg,
motion a fire underneath and bite your leg.
Lick the blood long. Look up and laugh, laugh!
Then take carrots, apples and oil, mash them
coated up to your arms, and wink the nearest goon
to come on up and sniff. Your tongue tells him
when he may lick, and just as they grow still.

Bite down, down, the blood, yick, the bite
curdling to puke, but stare them down, this
is crucial. Then let them laugh and make up
their own combinations: smearing an arm, a leg.
yellow, running around, and when they get

an audience, biting deep, deep. Ignore them.
Select quieter ones and finger in the sand
for them precise designs of other dishes.

A VOICE COLLAPSING

OK OK, so we look into dark,
out there, inside, sure we're alone.
So what, we got air, we got water and sod,
and look, nimble fingers! Yet we long
to take all time, death, and fear
and give it a mind. That way we're a plan
for ourselves to unravel. We rise
through our minds to see how we matter.
O we lift our light to a crazy bright!

Have you felt this real, felt it so right
it won't go away, then when you need it,
gone, it's gone? Take heart! Make up
a question and answer for something you
like. Babies? Sure. What do they dream?
And how did it feel the first time
Earth curved over for you, a ball
like your head spinning through what?

Are getting a feel? What opens the day?
You're swinging your arms. They are long.
Would you like my hat? It's on backwards
for fun. You're standing close. Do you
mind my voice? You won't find a thing
over there. I'm hungry. Sometimes I get
the hammers. We may have to wing it,
we may have to quit. You're not as short
as I thought. Please keep the hat.

A PLACE FOR FOUR-LETTER WORDS

I had it all wrong from the start
about four-letter words. I thought
they were big words with four letters.

I thought about being wrong.
I kept it quiet, cobweb quiet,
like our house, even our garage.

All but the shed where I kept
my bike. I looked for a place
to hear the words, all of them.

Before someone tried to tell me
where this one belonged and that
one didn't. Leaning streamlined

Over the handlebars, I heard them
in the tire's lick and spin. Faster,
tearing all out down a hill, hunched

Under the wind, blinking at the rain,
I yelled every four-letter word I knew,
yelled them until they were as real

As a hill, yelled them until I
broke them in the spokes and they were
just words spinning in the spokes.

THE TABLECLOTH EXPLANATION

It's all because the round man with the pumpkin neck
was teaching no one in particular macadam composition
and because a lady giggled like dry fire when the

bartender who liked lighting his lighter and looking
at it said a fellow wanted to be a vampire to get
the inside story but he had bad knees from football,

so he talked ladies into sponsoring a blood bank
and they all lounged in the blood bank lobby in
cracked leather chairs and sweep-around sunglasses,

gurgling, snoozing, bloated as ticks. Meanwhile,
I was sharpening my fork under the table,
under my napkin, humming over the ominous grating,

figuring one turn in the air maybe two, depending,
depending on the balance of the fork.
Thud a couple in the walls about ear high

to keep them at bay, but they charged me with chairs
and water-pitcher grenades and tied me up in these
tablecloths. I was badly outnumbered, officer.

THE MAN IN MY DREAMS

There's a man in my dreams I try to avoid.
He has a suitcase of skins. He zippers
himself into one, then another,

in bathrooms on trains, takes over
everyone I dream, even you, whom I envy
and plead with to take me over entirely,

to end this supposing someone else.
Do you understand? I mean, do you feel
at times like a motel? Do you wake in

the night to sounds of birds feeding?
I'm afraid of who I am. I dream
another, you, to believe in me.

VULTURE

Excuse me miss, but why do you stand so long
by this painting? Just because it's gilt framed
that doesn't make it a masterpiece. I know,
the vulture dismembering the rabbit is sad,
I suppose, but really it's funk sensationalism,
and I can see by your lovely paisley dress
that you have good taste. Is this for research?
Then note the theatrical light, the grand scale,
and how divorced the forest background is
from this macabre foreground scene.
Why then, may I ask, do you stand so close
and stare at the corner of the forest?

Oh, it's the girl in the back, in the white gown,
snarled and shrouded in the thorny matted foliage.
She seems transfixed, captured for an instant
by the horror of the rabbit's death,
and her face is like the face of the rabbit.
Rather morbid, but weird, yes, I see what
you mean: how can she just stand there and
scratch her back against the wet black bark?
Good point. How can she stand
before that apparition?—You know,
she seems almost to be purring and I feel
the beat of the vulture's wings as she purrs.
Yes, just like that, good for you!

THE DEEP LOVER OF MY BARBARA IS SILENCE

She tells me we are the love
she dreamed young when she gave
birds names. But when she fades

back, back, back, she's his.
He rolls her shoulders up
her neck. He dangles her lips

heavy off her mouth. I place
her feet in a bowl of water,
I take her hands and whisper

to gestures. I kiss her hands
and ask them to say hello
to her heart for me. I tell

her that her cat sinks
back into high grass like
a stream reversing. Come see,

let's go outside, it's lovely!
The names of flowers sing.
I'll name each flower you are to me!

HE COMES AS WIND

What if He comes disguised as air?
What if He wants to wander, to feel around
in what He's done, and comes as wind?

The people who bought a new something to wear,
are they to line up and be quiet?
The milling around, the short tempers,

And someone goading us on:
Look how the grass leans,
how the twigs are split open wide!

Yet the chill, just in the idea,
like the man there, is he shuddering
or is our anticipation quivering?

The wind may just be wind.
Then how do we appear to Him?
Listen, the wind is on us and gone.

And what if He comes without disguise?
Can we be with Him when He's here?
Does He let us imagine ourselves,

His way of kidding us along,
so that He can invent Himself again
in the notion: He comes as wind?

WE WENT DREAMING THE VALLEY
OF THE BLACK SOIL

We went dreaming the valley of the black soil,
across land we could have stayed in,
out there, always out there;
nights fell into each other, walking
was the only place to sleep.
We ended here where you're digging
but were gone before our bodies
opened to bones and our bones blazed,
even as sand they blazed—what can you do?
Down on your knees you dig and scrape
and clank. There, a busted tool
we threw away. You sigh over it.
You fondle worked rocks. You finger
everything, but your heart, could you heave
it up hill after hill, days of talking
to your feet, of walking so you won't
lie down; heave your heart
until the land below greens
and you eat out your eyes,
then pounce on the valley of the black soil,
eat it alive? Ha! you've never had to dream.

THE DARKNESS

Say you are out for a walk
and somewhere through the trees
you walk out of everything in your head

or off by a window in thought
and what you look out to
a crease of trees perhaps you don't see at all
but what you are thinking there in the trees

as you open like this through a window
or walk and walk into a gazing
then say darkness falls

darkness farther back than the cave you felt into
farther back than violence to animals

darkness farther back than water you dove into
hands in front of your face
to feel your way down and know
this darkness did not begin did not gather

then something backing off it seems as you come in
re-enters you and crosses you over
the sleep of the living and the dead

TOUR

The rumor among the houseboat locals
was that the old volcano was waking up mad
and its snorts were tossing tourists from canoes
—the ones who try to lick the moon off the water—
but tourists claimed the cove was full of mines.
Boats were outlawed and soon there were too many fish
for the tourists to enjoy swimming,
so to lure the rush into huge nets
the resort owners dribbled garbage into the cove
and flattered their guests into doing fancy casting
from the balconies and the cocktail veranda.

Sharks tailed in after the fish,
then rolled in shallow for the garbage
and shadowed the wading area.
The resort owners led a posse to the boats
and chased the sharks around the cove,
shooting at them and now and then
at one another just for fun and also
to keep down the drinking and dozing in the boats
until the mines went up, toppling all the resorts,
and that is why this lovely seaside village
is not included on this year's tour. However,
our bus makes a rest stop on the corniche boulevard
where they still sell last year's postcards.

I FIRST PRACTICED PICKING UP SMALL THINGS

I first practiced picking up small things
with my toes. Then I hung from trees
and in a couple of weeks I got good
at looking around upside down.
Headstands at home helped. I worked
hard too on the soft drop to ground,
then added coming up into a four legged
shuffle, and on up into a hunched run.
Next I mastered the spin around bellow.
I was ready to leave the backyard.
I took to the fields and let fly
with swoopers. These I had practiced
nights in my room. You swing your arms
and wind them so that your shoulders
roll. This adds a lope to your run.
I got into a swooper after a soft
drop from a tree and up through
a four legged shuffle to my hunched
run. The dogs weren't my idea
and that's when the neighbors
said they were going to lasso me,
hobble me in a corral, but I knew
they were just making fun because
there aren't any corrals around.
I was excited and then I realized
cars are a lot older and wilder
than we think. Perhaps we tamed them
too much. Anyway I want to emancipate

cars. A big idea and since you all
have one I thought I should ask you
first. I'm serious or I wouldn't
come here to our town meeting.

BARGAIN

I got 2 marriages 1 wife 1 mother
2 stepchildren 1 secretary 1 job
2 sons 2 houses 3 cars 1 daughter
1 school board 1 civic post 3 clubs
3 bank accounts 1 dog 1 boat 9 credit
cards 3 charities and the 4th tax bracket.

That gives me a total of 42. That means,
Arthur, you're 1st with 58. I buy
your martinis for a month on this train.
Toby, your 39 is 3rd. You throw in
3 days of your vacation and drive
a cab, working out of the town station.

Bruce, your 37 makes you last man.
You go to an island for a week, alone,
doing nothing. When you return
you can't tell anyone anything.

AMERICAN HERO: A POEM MADE INTO A MOVIE

Silhouetted on a ledge, the grand beast known
in local legend as the Vanilla Gorilla! My posse
tumbles like dominoes. I take my fiberglass bow,
lay an arrow in, and vissst!—my arrow snips
him off, punctures his little ear so bulbous red
it looks inside out. He goes dummy on the ledge,
tips over. People want hair, clumps of it, parades,
a national holiday. Cubs, Brownies, Legionnaires,
and Miss American Aphrodite sipping warm milk
with nuns and the DAR, and girls with skin
like bubble gum, dancing the squid, the tongue,
the pneumatic drill. I'm led to a reviewing stand
where a retired WAC called Sizzles proclaims me
"Hero!" and a bear of a jukebox rolls to my chest
swelling. My heartbeat is recorded for the country.

I run for the woods, hug a tree. Something gives.
I want to be a crowd. My feet feel like galoshes.
There's Miss American Aphrodite! She's the girl
next door, girl with parents, girl with other guy.
She stares at her drink. Her ice is melting.
I feel as big as a ranch. She's coming up,
I hear her bubbling. Her face is a swimming pool.
I want to be a helicopter, hover over her, dangle
my arms to her. We go for a spin, run every light
and go the wrong way up a one-way. Faster,

faster. Water running down a sink. Grab
for the soap. Save the soap. Forget the soap.
We hit the drain with the sound of a kiss.

NIGHT GOLF

We tee off under the moon
and walk into my first hole of Night Golf.
My ball is nowhere. I drop another ball
and send a seam along the dark.
This ball I lose too. I like the swat,
the moon night tingling, but I will lose
no more balls. I pretend, I swing
on a ball I imagine. My friends stroll over
and say I am picking up the game fast.
Thanks loads, I reply. At the top of my backswing
I see myself naked. I laugh,
go to my knees. My friends laugh with me.
I try again, I swing without a club
and walk under the ball
I see floating to the green. There,
I stroke a long putt, my head down
over my follow through. I don't keep score.
There's no score in Night Golf.
You swing and look your ball into the dark.
You walk with friends across land you don't know,
saying little, allowing your stride
to find a softness you vaguely recall.
You may go far with yourself,
far, and be content by morning.
If not, the day floats until the moon rises.

DODO BIRDS

The lug shakes himself awake like a duck,
this eyewash who hit the party as if he just
got in from both coasts. His wife who talks

to feel her quiver lips move, tiptoes around
every guy here, then passes out with her hand
in the ashtray and a shag of hair cupped

over her left breast. It ends on the way down
around the ice box, something about bushes too
near the drive. Shadows shadows. They can't

drive, I can't sleep. That's fate and fried
eggs, coffee, house apologies and a tall shot
to get me home to hate, better each night,

what I've done and haven't,
like the next day, not me up for me again,
lugging my bed slab of a body to the sink.

O feel the hulk blood up, the whole rubber
tree frame flapping again, with step so sure
it goes where the eye sights down a pant leg.
If anyone asks at work, I'm a house of hair.

HANDS

My hands can't forget you being here.
They fiddle. I rub them above my eyes,
crinkle the skin down over and close
my eyes deeper on you moving away.
Where are you thinking of now?
You have so many places you could be
here, and take my hands again as if
you we taking them with you
and swing them as if they could fly.
You said I looked good. What did I say?
My hands, they fiddle, and grind.
When will I be like you, so easily here,
saying you dropped in and will again?
Then I can let you go easily and
my hands can open in a deep breath.

BOTTOMING OUT

Driving at night and my lights go out
at sixty. I'm wired wide-eyed
yelling inside miles away that won't
be here. I'm here, be here, the car's blind!
The brake? No, I'd be piled from behind,

Their lights liquid in the back window.
The lights in front I freeze on. The dark
must have a zipper. No, I'm doing a gawk
skin and bone right out to zero.
Get off the road! Gun it, now slow, slow,

And stop. Believe ground. The dead
eyes, kick them into the dashboard.
Kick the holes. Carlights swish over like
huge slow bullets. I lift my hands
into them. Hands want to cleat bark.

I rush a tree, chip off bark.
It tastes like hair rolled for days
and glued. I want to pry myself open,
lift the spine out whole, pull it back
like a bow, set my head in,
and fire my head away.

AT THE COAST

I look up—there in the motel glass door
I sit opposite myself, the night to my back,
the ocean rolling. I look through myself
into trees halfway up the moon.

A wave cracks, tears across the break.
Another breath I'm down the dune path
out on the long backwash
that drags the low beach clean.

Why aren't you here? You love this glaze
of water. With one touch
you could have it shining. What can I give up
that I'm not already losing?

ACKNOWLEDGMENTS

The author wishes to thank the editors of the following publications in which some of the poems in this volume originally appeared:

Apercus: "The Problem of Being a Pallbearer in this City Under Siege," "Dear Giant Squid #2," "The Old Demon Drops By to Cool Off"

The Antioch Review: "Slip Away"

Aspen Anthology: "Dear Mrs. Sears"

The Atlantic: "Oil Spill"

Beloit Poetry Journal: "American Hero: A Poem Made into a Movie"

Black Warrior Review: "Green Diver"

Chowder Review: "We Went Dreaming the Valley of Black Soil"

Colorado State Review: "Openers," "A Voice Collapsing," "The Deep Lover of My Barbara is Silence"

Continental Drift: "Halloween of the Sudden Hand"

Corduroy: "At the Coast"

The Cortland Review: "No Problem," "It's Shifts of Sideways if She Talks to You"

Field: "To a Young Woman Considering Suicide"

Hanging Loose: "Bargain," "Taking On a Goon of Death"

High Desert Journal: "Worried Sick in Klamath Falls"

Hubbub: "My Time May Come at Any Time," "Do Not Let Them Take Me Away if Naked," "Like a Spot in the Woods where the Deer Slept"

Ksor Guide to the Arts: "You'll Have to Stay for Lunch and there is No Lunch"

Let Us Drink to the River: An Anthology of River Poems: "Night Fishing"

Many Mountains Moving: "Some of the Dead Go to the City"

Mead: "Even in Hades they Talk Turkey"

Mother Jones: "Big Shot Graces the Old Bar & Grill," "Hands," "Bottoming Out"

Night Out: Poems about Hotels, Motels, Restaurants, and Bars: "Harvey Wallbanger"

Northwest Literary Forum: "Coming Home"

Northwest Review: "The Brink," "What Scared Me as a Boy was not My Sex"

The Oregonian: "Valentine," "I'm on a Small Ledge below a Peak," "Chemo Silver"

Oregon Literary Review: "What Grandfather Did at his Funeral," "When the Red Wind Blows," "My Emptiness Rides in the Back Seat, Propped Up"

Orion: "Snow at Night"

Phantom Drift: "At the Old Cemetery Outside Fossil"

Poet & Critic: "Standing Water"

Poetry Bay: "Hey Chuck," "When I Listen in my Car to Mozart's 'Don Giovanni'"

Poetry Northwest: "How do you Really Do?' "Grandfather and the Rabbit," "Vulture"

Poetry Now: "Moon Gliding," "I'll Give you Fall and Winter," "The Man in my Dreams," "He Comes as Wind"

Portland Alliance: "Collateral Damage"

Portland Review: "The Lady Who Got me to Say So Long Mom," "It's in the Eyes"

Premiere: "Dodo Birds"

Prescott Street Reader: "Bad Day"

Rhino: "His Friend the Beast"

Saturday Review: "A Place for Four Letter Words," "Tour"

Seattle Review: "I Won't Need Legs There"

Seneca Review: "The Darkness"

Silk Road: "The Little Trees are Older than I Am"

Southern Poetry Review: "Brother"

Upstart: "Bike Run," "Escape from East Berlin"

Willow Springs: "Birds that Beat the Sky to Bits," "I Might Break, I Might Disappear," "Full Heat that Flutters"

Write Corner Press: "Morning Light," "Back from War"

Writer's Dojo Literary Journal: "Clouds Roll over the Mountains Like so Many Little Hills"

Xanadu: "Man on a Bicycle"

Yes Poetry: "The Foam Machine"

Zyzzyva: "Traffic Jam on the Ross Island Bridge"

Additionally, "Plane Down in Moriches Bay" appeared in *Poets of the American West*, ed. Lowell Jaeger, Many Voices Press (Kalispell, MT) 2010.

I would like to thank Dave Jarecki and John Morrison. I would also like to thank Judith Barrington, Kurt Brown, Robin Cody, Barbara Drake, Barbara LaMorticella, Michael Malan, John A. Miller, Paulann Petersen, John Rember, Joanna Rose, Vern Rutsala, and Penelope Scambly Schott.